A Set Time in Your Life

by John Henry

TRILOGY

A Set Time in Your Life

Trilogy Christian Publishers A Wholly Owned Subsidary of Trinity Broadcasting Network

2442 Michelle Drive Tustin, CA 92780

Copyright © 2021 by John Henry

Cover design by: Natalee Dunning

Rights Department, 2442 Michelle Drive, Tustin, CA 92780.

Trilogy Christian Publishing/TBN and colophon are trademarks of Trinity Broadcasting Network.

For information about special discounts for bulk purchases, please contact Trilogy Christian Publishing.

Trilogy Disclaimer: The views and content expressed in this book are those of the author and may not necessarily reflect the views and doctrine of Trilogy Christian Publishing or the Trinity Broadcasting Network.

Manufactured in the United States of America

10 9 8 7 6 5 4 3 2 1

Library of Congress Cataloging-in-Publication Data is available.

ISBN: 978-1-64773-271-4

E-ISBN: 978-1-64773-272-1

DEDICATION

I dedicate this book to my family and friends that love the Lord and cannot wait to see Him; the Lord has a time set for His coming that no one can change. We must believe in Him and also in the Bible and acknowledge it has the word of God. The Bible is also a map to direct us to a destination where we can receive eternal life.

Finally, I dedicate this book to all the people who lost loved ones, families, friends from coronavirus disease; my heart and prayers go out to you. With the word of prophet Isaiah, I affirm, "Fear thou not; for I am with thee: be not dismayed; for I am thy God: I will strengthen thee; yea, I will help thee; yea, I will uphold thee with the right hand of my righteousness" (Isaiah 41:10, KJV). God promised to take care of you.

ACKNOWLEDGMENTS

Writing a book is harder than I thought and more rewarding than I could have ever imagined. None of this would have been possible without the support of my family.

With a heart full of praise to God and thanksgiving to His people, I want to acknowledge the following individuals:

- My wife, Novlette Henry, who took the time to offer moral and spiritual support.
- My son, Jevonte Henry, who, although a teenager, dedicated his time to help.
- My beautiful daughter, Shevaunia Henry, who helped me keep my faith in the Lord.
- The staff of Trilogy Professional Publishing for their willingness and hard work. Their prayers and skillful work helped publish this book.

The book *A Set Time in Your Life* took over two years to write. I pray that it will be a blessing to many people throughout their Christian walk with the Lord.

TABLE OF CONTENTS

INTRODUCTION

I was almost eighteen years old when I said these words: "I will never get the chance to enter the United States of America because there is no one to help me." My mother and father were still living in Jamaica, West Indies, so I prayed and let the Lord know how I felt. I can remember I was attentively watching all my friends and their families going back and forth from the United States of America—it seems like it was yesterday. At the same time, I was filling out applications and looking for jobs. Day after day, I was going to different businesses and was to complete more applications. One day, one of my good friends gave me an application to work on a cruise ship. I completed the application and gave it back to my friend. It was hard to find a job in those days. The only option was to learn a trade. After learning a trade and mastering it, I started my own business.

In January 1990, I was in my place of business when I heard someone call, "Mr. Henry!" I took a look, and to my surprise, I saw a large Caucasian man looking at me. I was surprised because the only time you would see a white person in my neighborhood was when driving through the neighborhood. At the same time, all the children in the neighborhood were gathered around him as if they had never seen a white person before. The man handed me some papers with instructions. He also told me that I had to leave within the next two weeks. He said, "Your flight is paid, and the ship captain expects your arrival at a certain time." Just to let you know how God works: after all this time when I was looking for a job, God just opened a door in my life that no one could close. This is my inspiration for the title of this book, *A Set Time in Your Life*.

The Bible tells us about a man called Lazarus; he was a beggar, always at the gate of the rich man. Lazarus was full of sores all over his body; the dogs would come and lick him. When the rich man ate and the crumbs fell from the rich man's table, Lazarus would eat them. Luke 16:22 (KJV) says, "And it came to pass, that the beggar died, and was carried by the angels into Abraham bosom: the rich man also died, and was buried." Both men died; Lazarus went to heaven, and the rich man went to hell. I would like to encourage the reader: in this life on the earth, we may face persecution, but the Lord says He will prepare a place in eternity for us. The rich man was so tormented in hell he cried out to Abraham to send Lazarus to dip the tip of his finger with water and cool the man's tongue (Luke 16:24). We may achieve earthly things, but those things cannot go to heaven; only our soul will enter heaven. Mark 8:36 (KJV) says, "For what shall it profit a man, if he shall gain the whole world, and lose his own soul?" Lazarus was poor on the earth but rich in heaven. His time has come.

A SET TIME

Many people around the world today are praying for a better life, but their time has not yet come. However, when their time comes, no one will be able to stop them. God wants us to enjoy everything that He put on the earth. If we stay in prayer, He will answer it one day. The evil one will try to step in and deny God's people their legacy. God makes promises to us that He will never leave us or forsake us. There is a time coming—a set time—a time that God ordained to give back to His children all that the cankerworms and caterpillars have eaten.

God always encourages us to take one day at a time because He knows everything before it happens. Some people do not know that God created everything. He sets things up, and He breaks things down. Blessed is the name of the Lord. As children of the Most High King, we will go through problems. However, Psalm 30:5 (KJV) states, "For His anger endureth but a moment; in his favour is life: weeping may endure for a night, but joy cometh in the morning." No man on earth can stop you, and that is a set time in your life.

When Moses ran away from Egypt, he was just relaxing at the back side of the desert, but one day, while he was cooling off, the Lord appeared to him and gave him the assignment to go back to Egypt. Brothers and sisters, I am talking about a set time.

Sometimes, we do something wrong in the church or to someone in the church. The pastor says something to us, and we respond by saying words that do not fit with the character of a child of God and choose not to go back to the church. God wants to bless us in the church, but when we behave in such a way, we delay God's blessings and lose our set time with God. What we need to do is learn how to recognize when God is present and at work. We never know when God will show up. The Bible tells us that God often reveals Himself to people in the most unexpected ways.

Ecclesiastes 3:1-8 (KJV) says,

> To everything there is a season, and a time to every purpose under the heaven: A time to be born, and a time to die; a time to plant, and a time to pluck up that which is planted; A time to kill, and a time to heal; a time to break down, and a time to build up; A time to weep, and a time to laugh; a time to mourn, and a time to dance; A time to cast away stones, and a time to gather stones together; a time to embrace, and a time to refrain from embracing; A time to get and a time to lose; a time to keep, and a time to cast away; A time to rend, and a time to sew; a time to keep silence, and a time to speak; A time to love, and a time to hate; a time of war, and a time of peace.

When God made this world, He did that in His time. Human beings do not like to wait. Sometimes, we cry out to God, "When is my time?" "Why are so many bad things happening to me?" "Why can't I get a breakthrough?" Despite our feelings of longing and despair, all we have to do is stay in line because there is a time coming when no one can stop us, and that is our time. I can remember times in my own life when God made a way for me by sending just the right people, the ones who could tell me the next step to take in finding Him or who could help me work out some major things, especially when I was trying to become a minister.

One of the people God sent to help me was the pastor of my church. His name is Lloyd Phipps. Without him, I don't know what I would have done. I am always asking God to send someone to help me with preaching because I am a young minister. One night, Lloyd asked me to minister to the people, and after I finished speaking,

I went to him, and he said, "I think there is room for growth." He told me how to structure my sermon. I prayed night and day to God for someone, and that night He sent me help.

When I reached out to God for help, He provided it. God was able to bring someone to teach me exactly what I needed at that time. God will always be there for you. When God called Moses to go back to Egypt to bring out the Israelites, Moses came up to the Red Sea. Moses did not know what to do because the pharaoh and his army were coming. God told Moses, "But lift thou up thy rod, and stretch out thine hand over the sea, and divide it: and the children of Israel shall go on dry ground through the midst of the sea" (Exodus 14:16, KJV). Sometimes, it seems so hard to us, but remember: He is God. There is no problem too hard for Him. Isaiah 40:31 (KJV) says, "But they that wait upon the LORD shall renew their strength; they shall mount up with wings as eagles; they shall run, and not be weary; and they shall walk, and not faint." To all the young people out there: never give up, pray to the Lord for help in everything that you are about to do, and He will give you direction.

This Is Your Time

A good friend of mine by the name of Wesley married his high-school girlfriend by the name of Judith. The couple engaged in business; they opened a clothing store. The business was very successful. Wesley and Judith were planning to buy their dream house. The couple was blessed with two beautiful children. Everything was going well. One day, Judith suspected that Wesley was cheating and hanging out with some friends who were involved in drugs. Wesley started to use and sell drugs. As a result, the family was being devastated. It was a sunny day in June when the police called the house to inform Judith that her husband was in jail.

Judith did not know what to do. The first thing that came to her mind was to bail Wesley out. Judith went to the police station, and the officer told her that Wesley was also using drugs. Judith was upset; she paid the bail with the money that was put aside for the house. The couple's dream took a bad turn. All the money from the business was depleted.

One day, as I was about to start dinner, my phone rang. Wesley was on the other line. We talked for hours. As we were about to finish, I asked Wesley to ask God to break the old ways of doing things by human willpower and reach out to God with an open mind. I prayed for Wesley, asking God to perform a miracle. Wesley kept on saying, "There is no treatment facility that will understand me or my faith or be able to help me overcome my addiction," but he said he was open to God's help. When he said those words, I started giving God praise. I felt something move inside my body. I said, "The miracle started." Judith turned to me and said, "I know exactly where to take him. The next day, Judith called up a drug rehabilitation center. Her plan was to take her husband back from the devil. The drug had an instant grip on Wesley, and this respectful businessman had suddenly found himself to be something that he had never imagined. Wesley would never have imagined himself being an addict. Can you think for a moment how incredibly conflicting that must have been for someone who previously thought that addicts were people who hang out in alleys or run-down buildings? Judith told Wesley, "Unfortunately, you are in the grips of a powerful substance." Judith told Wesley no human being must play with a powerful substance like a drug because those powerful substances distress many powerful human beings.

Sometimes, it takes one thing to happen in the family: a member develops a bad sickness. As a result, all the members of that family start to attend the local church in their neighborhood. Judith thought that going to church would erase all their problems. Going to church will never erase your problems. Make a commitment to God and stay under the cross because there is a time coming—a set time—and only God can give you that time. In John 5:4, there was a man with an infirmity, waiting to get in the water when an angel came down and troubled the water, but there was no one to help him. One day, while the man was there, Jesus stopped by and said, "Wilt thou be made whole? "(John 5:6, KJV). I am talking about a set time; no one could stop this man at that time.

Judith said Wesley finished his recovery program at the rehabilitation center and went back into the family business. They purchased their dream house and sent their two children to college. Sometimes, it seems like our dreams make some wrong turns, but when God is the driver, all we have to do is keep our seat belt fastened and enjoy the ride.

God's Time Is Different from the World's Time

Chances are that few people who are reading this book have reached a place in life and believe they are beyond the need for God's help and grace. Chance is that you believe you are a normal person living a reasonably normal life. Yes, you may think you are normal, but I have read about some normal people in my life. Remember Solomon: he also thought he was normal; he had everything, he was rich, and he had a lot of girls. But one day, when his heart ministered to him, he cried out to God for help and testified and said all these things are vanity. Ecclesiastes 1:2 (KJV) says, "Vanity of vanities, saith the Preacher; vanity of vanities, all is vanity." What is normal? In fact, most people who think that they are normal often feel there is still something missing in their lives. You may have everything, but there is a time coming, a set time, that everything you have may be taken away from you.

The only thing that will stand in your relationship with God is love. God wants your life to be better, so He sent His only Son to die for you. A good relationship first starts with God. In order for us to go forward in life, we must love the people that hurt us. It is not easy, but it is the will of God. In order for you to have a relationship with God, you have to show love. Matthew 22:37 (KJV) says, "Jesus said unto him, thou shalt love the Lord thy God with all thy heart, and with all thy soul, and with all thy mind." When you say that you love God, you must think about it because if you say you love God, you cannot hate your brother. You cannot see God, but you see your brother every day. First John 4:7 (KJV) says, "Beloved, let us love one another: for love is of God; and every one that loveth is born of God, and knoweth God."

How to Enjoy Marriage

When Ethan and Destiny got married, they were the most loving and romantic couple I had ever seen. If you saw Ethan walking to the store, Destiny would be coming behind; they were always together. The couple took vacations together. They also visited family members together; when Destiny told Ethan that she was pregnant, he was so happy. Destiny's pregnancy took a bad turn: she started to get sick every day, and she was in and out of the hospital. Ethan started to come home late at night because he would be hanging out with a friend. One night, Destiny stopped Ethan by the door and asked him, "What is going on with you?" Ethan told her that he did not know that married life was so hard. Destiny told Ethan that their marriage was young and he should give more time to the marriage. "You are acting like a bachelor, coming late at night, taking a vacation by yourself. Time can change everything; give it some time, and God will help you get to the place in your marriage between where you are in life and where you want to be." Destiny told Ethan, "You thought marriage is like reading a love book. It can be, but God has to be the center of that marriage." Ephesians 5:25 (KJV) says, "Husbands, love your wives, even as Christ also loved the church, and gave himself for it."

Destiny told Ethan, "It's about your personal goals: finish law school and be the best lawyer in town. All the accomplishments are good, but remember: there is a baby on the way. We must work together and pray to the Lord for this baby to be born in good health." Ethan started to cry and apologized to Destiny, "I am so sorry; I did not see it that way. All I was thinking about was fulfilling my dreams and leaving a legacy for my family." With all the sickness that Destiny went through, God blessed her with a beautiful baby girl. Ethan thanks Destiny every day for the correction in his life. Destiny replies to him, "I forgive you," and they are about to get baptized in the church. You must be careful not to become stuck in this gap with personal patterns, the way you want things to be done. It is good for you to have things done your way; patience can help you not to become annoyed and anxious. Remember, the Bible says, "Delight thyself also in the Lord; and he shall give thee the desires of thine heart" (Psalm 37:4, KJV).

God Opened Doors

Yes, time changes everything, but we put in some work so that God can move in the situation. God keeps telling us that He loves us (1 John 4:7, 11). Remember, we cannot generate this love; it must come through the Holy Spirit. When we pray to God to use us, sometimes, He takes us through the fire in the same way that He did with Joseph so you may stand out on top of your enemy. God's sovereignty, love, and mercy are unbelievable. He can take us to places that we've never been before. It's so amazing to look back into your life and see how far God has brought you. Now, you are a pastor, doctor, lawyer, minister, and the list goes on. You didn't think you could make it, but God opened the door for you, and no one could stop you because God ordained that time for you. I am talking about a set time.

The reason God put you on top is to empower you and use you. You may have money, but God does not want your money. You may have influence, but that is not what God wants. He plucked you out of this world and out of the hands of the enemy so He could develop intimacy with you. That intimacy is not to make you feel good about yourself but to make others know about Him. Come to Him with open arms, and He will forgive you of your sin. "Blessed is he whose transgression is forgiven, whose sin is covered. Blessed is the man unto whom the LORD imputeth not iniquity, and in whose spirit there is no guile" (Psalm 32:1-2, KJV).

Help Someone

Sometimes, you are unable to change ways of thinking and living that defeat your best efforts. When Kevin and Taylor started dating, they were from different cultural backgrounds: he was from Jamaica, West Indies, and she was from Africa. They do things differently, like the way they cook, Kevin likes fried food, and Taylor likes baked food. It was a problem, so the couple decided to go to the pastor for counseling. Taylor told the pastor that fried food is bad for Kevin. Kevin said, "I can understand what she is saying, but give me some time. Romans 14:3 (KJV) says, "Let not him that eateth despise him that eateth not; and let not him which eateth not judge him that eateth; for God hath received him. To change that pattern, you need to give that person some time and pray with him or her because time changes everything." Taylor says, "Yes, time changes everything, but we need to put in some work so that God can move in the situation."

We must not pressure someone to change on our time; pray for that person and put the situation in God's hands. There is nothing too hard that the Lord cannot do: He opened the Red Sea. We, as human beings, will have problems, but God will help us on the way and deliver us out of them. Kevin came to understand that if a change is going to take place, God is to do it because he is limited. First Peter 5:7 (KJV) says, "Casting all your care upon Him; for He careth for you." Kevin and Taylor prayed to the Lord for help, and both of them started to eat healthier. Because the couple gave up their bad eating habit, they decided to open a restaurant and help other people to eat good food.

Sometimes, God will let things happen in your life for you to get your true potential unleashed. Kevin and Taylor have one of the biggest health food restaurants in California. God will let things happen in your life just to let you achieve the blessing He has for you. And that is a set time in your life.

You Want to Change Time

May people put off the decision to commit their lives to serve God? My pastor told a story about a lady who visited the church one Sunday morning. After the pastor preached, there was an altar call. The lady went to the altar, and the pastor talked to her about Christ. She told the pastor that she was not ready. One day, she called her ex-boyfriend for money for their child. He told her to come for it, and as she entered the door, he chopped her up.

The time is now. Do not wait. Remember when your parents used to take you to church? Now, you're a grown-up and are trying to recapture the wonder of that childlike faith you had when you were younger. The Bible tells us in Psalm 144:12, "That our sons may be as plants grown up in their youth; that our daughters may be as corner stones, polished after the similitude of a palace." You cannot change time. Put the past behind you and go forward to make that connection with God. You know He loves you, and He will accept you and give you the best. You can also restore your spiritual relationship with Him. Some religious people will judge you. Remember the lady with the blood problem? She did not waste time. The first chance she got, she held on to His garment, and from that day, she was healed. The Lord takes care of His people, but at the same time, we have a job to be done. She did not stay at home and cry about her sickness; she stepped out and exercised her faith in the Lord. Psalm 13:5-6 (KJV) says, "But I have trusted in thy mercy; my heart shall rejoice in thy salvation. I will sing unto the Lord because he hath dealt bountifully with me."

Everyone says they have faith in God, but as problems come their way, they start to question God, "Why me?" Sometimes, there is a reason you are facing that problem. It comes to make you strong. "Faith is the substance of things hoped for, the evidence of things not seen" (Hebrews 11:1, KJV). Faith is the victory that overcomes the world, and without faith, it is impossible to please God. Remember, when Abram took Isaac to be killed for a burnt offering, God provided a lamb. God saw the faith in Abram. How many of us are willing to sacrifice our son? Not many, but Abram knew the God he servedAbram's faith was both in attitude and in action. Because of Abram's faith, God gave him the title of the father of the nations and made a covenant with him. We must be faithful to God because there is a reward in heaven for us.

Galatians 2:16 (KJV) says,

> Knowing that a man is not justified by the works of the law, but by the faith of Jesus Christ, even we have believed in Jesus Christ, that we might be justified by the faith of Christ, and not by the works of the law.

The more you act on your faith in God, the more you will see His way for you. It is an active, not passive, process because God is active on your behalf, even when you cannot see it. God also calls you to be active. I do not think you are reading this book by coincidence. This time was set by God for you to read this book. I believe that you will have the same experience as Abram when you exercise your faith in God by following the principles that God gave to Abram.

Start Your Journey with God's Time

I can remember the first day when I started to work on a tourist boat. The sun was shining. It seemed like nothing could go wrong. To my surprise, I met some longtime friends from my school days. We talked for over an hour. I made a statement like, "This job is the best thing that could happen to me." Coming to acknowledge everything that I was saying, I realize that with the love of God, we let Him take us to a place where we have never been before. When everything was placed in the right perspective, I realized that God's time is different; He has a plan for my life. This job was a journey for me to travel around the world. I was able to see things I had never seen before. It helped me appreciate things more because I was on God's time. I would like you to know that, whenever you are on a journey with God, there are some things you would like to do and some places you would like to go, but God has His own destination and time where He wants to place you.

God place Jesus on the boat (Mark 4: 37KJV) say and there arose a great storm of wind, and the waves beat into the ship, so that it was now full. Jesus was going over on the other side of the sea, but it was a great storm of wind. The devil knows that there was a demon possess man that dwell among the tombs. So, he tries to stop Jesus' form going over there the devil did not want Jesus to heal the possess man. Sometime the Lord place us into some place and position in life for a reason. God place me on that tourist boat so I can minster to many of the worker from different country some of them have no knowledge of God. They ask many question the one question that stay in my head is every Christian believe in God.

Actually, in one sense, what he said was true. Meany people who are Christians and attend church have difficulty believing in God. A lot of them are confused and do not know what he or she believes in, especially when a member of their family gets sick or dies. In the Bible, Jesus told some of the people who were following Him that they were not following Him because of the preaching but because of the fish and bread.

What I would assert to us today is that it is much better to serve God than man. It is not that belief will make time. It is that God will make the time to take us to heaven. Belief and faith are the steps of trust that we take to connect us to the real God who makes the time for us. You may recall the story of Hannah from the Bible. God closed her womb, but when she prayed and asked God to remember her, God gave her a son. She named him Samuel. Eli accused her of being drunk, but she replied to Eli, "I am not drunk. I am a woman who is going through a problem." I am writing this book to reach the heart of someone who is going through a lot in life. Just ask God to help you.

He did it for Hannah, and He can also do it for you. Just have faith and keep on believing in the God who made heaven and earth. I just want to give a friend hope and courage to get through a rough time or reach a goal. The problem in life is that we all are in similar situations, but God will help us. Hannah could not do anything to open her womb, but she had faith and belief in God. Romans 4:5 (KJV) says, "But to him that worketh not, but believeth on him that justifieth the ungodly, his faith is counted for righteousness."

Just imagine how Hannah feel she pray to God year after year for a child and no answer but one day, a set time God answer her pray. Hannah knows that she has nothing to do with it, so she talks with God and give the child back to God. Samuel changes the hold aspect of His generation he anointed people to be king. Psalm 107:9 (KJV) says, "For he satisfieth the longing soul, and filleth the hungry soul with goodness."

A Time When You Are Down

When Moses was taking the Israelites out of Egypt, they came upon the Red Sea, and everyone was down. God knew about this before Moses was born. This time was set and waiting for Moses to come to start this work. There was no one on the earth who could set this up but one man, and He is the father of all men, the Lord. The fact that you and I need someone greater than ourselves is not a weakness. Many people say that our need for God is like a woman who is in childbirth: as soon as the child is delivered, the mother forgets the pain. Some people try to use God. When some people get sick, and you pray with them, they give you the most amazing story: "As soon as the sickness lives my body, I will come to church with you," but they keep on putting it off. The Bible says in Philippians 4:4 (KJV): "Rejoice in the Lord always: and again I say, Rejoice."

Humans were created and designed to take care of the outside of themselves to find the things that they need each day. The biggest problem some people have is when they achieve things in life, they brag about it. No man nor woman can ever achieve things in life unless God allows it. There was a friend of mine by the name of Pam. She came to America with just her clothes on her back. She worked two jobs; she purchased her first house in a good neighborhood and bought a car. She started to look down on her friends; she bragged about her house and money. She caught COVID-19 in the company where she was working; the company closed down. Pam never got the chance to work with any more companies again; the bank took back the house, and she is staying with her family. We must remember that we pass on the way up the people that we will see on the way down.

Life was designed to let us know sometimes we are going down, but when we trust in God, we have hope. We did not make ourselves, to begin with, nor did we design life and how it is supposed to go. I would say to some people out there: life has its up and downs. When you fall, do not stay down. I always tell myself I am like water: you plug here, and I burst out somewhere else because I am unstoppable.

Remember David from the Bible: he went down so many times but picked himself up; he was anointed to become a king, but he never went on the throne right away. He had to fight battles. I am just here to encourage my readers: when things get hard, please do not give up. Stay in the race and put up a fight. God knows that we can help ourselves in difficult times because there is something in you and me that God put in us for us to go through hard times. Remember that life is a journey, and the first step of realizing, since you are not God, is by experiencing some problem in this flesh. Job 14:1 (KJV) states, "Man that is born of a woman is of few days and full of trouble." You were put on this earth to serve God.

Many parents try to create a lifestyle for their child, and most of the time, it creates a problem. We, parents, need to go to God in prayer and ask Him what our children desire. Sometimes, kids want to live their life the way God intended for them to live. Remember when the Lord said, "Suffer little children to come unto me, and forbid them not: for of such is the kingdom of God (Luke 18:16, KJV). He was talking about all the children. Kids will make mistakes, but with God as their shepherd, they could live a life in a relationship with the true and living God. God knows what is best for His children, and He will supply it to them.

This is what I am talking about: trials and problems in your life. There is a time coming when God says it is over; it is your time now. No one can stop you. This is a set time in your life.

How to Depend on God

Instead of talking to God about our problems, we need to ask Him what we can do when we do not know what to do. Some people try to solve their problems by themselves, but they just keep on repeating them over and over again. Some of us try very hard to serve the Lord, but we cannot do it by ourselves. God has to do it through us. Romans 7:21 (ESV) says, "So I find it to be a law that when I want to do right, evil lies close at hand." Every human being has to depend on God if they want to engage in a relationship with the Most High God. Some say, "This time, it will be different because this time, I am making a sincere commitment with Him." I try to let people know: in order for you to go forward in God, prayer has to be on your tongue night and day.

The approach some people take to serve God is not good; there is only one way to serve the Lord. The main problem some of us have is we refuse to dedicate our life to the Lord. We must remember the life we are living is not ours; it is God's life. He gave it to you, and He will take it away from you. A good friend of mine by the name of Bob told me he was not partying anymore, so he decided to start coming to church on Sunday. On two Sundays, he was missing. I tried to call him but got no answer, so one day, I went to his house. He was sleeping; he woke up with his face looking so bad. He told me he went out with some friends and got stoned. I prayed with him right there, and I asked him if he would come to church on Sunday, and he replied, "I will try."

About five weeks later, a member of his family told me he went out with some friends again, and one of them tried to poison him. He was in the hospital fighting for his life; he was also drunk. Bob did not know how much God was keeping him when he left the presence of the Lord and gave the devil room to come in. Sometimes, when we leave our house, we do not know God has His angels around us because we cannot see them. Second Kings 6:16 (KJV) says Elisha said to his servant, "Fear not: for they that be with us are more than they that be with them," but he could not see them. God takes care of His people. Many people are born with sickness in their bodies, and the doctor gave them over to die. Despite the doctor's diagnosis, they live to be seventy-five years old. We need to realize who God is. We cannot solve the problems that face us in life. We do not have the answer to every question in life. But one thing I know is He promised to never leave us or forsake us.

Sometimes, we try to do things our way, and that is the biggest mistake we make. Proverbs 3:5-6 (NIV) says, "Trust in the Lord with all your heart and lean not on your own understanding; in all your ways submit to Him, and He will make your paths straight." If you would like to open a ministry, go to God in prayer, and He will make your paths straight. God loves us so much that if we just ask, He will make a way for us. I can remember when I was looking for a job, I was tired of going on interviews; I almost gave up. I was at home, telling myself I was not going on more interviews. One day, while I was driving to the store, I happened to see a fleet of trucks, so I decided to stop and talk to the boss. I went inside and asked the supervisor if the company was hiring drivers; he told me, "Yes, would you like to start right now?" I was so surprised I did not know what to say. I told the supervisor, "Can I start tomorrow because my wife is waiting for the food to cook for dinner?" I can remember reading the Bible, Matthew 7:7 (KJV), when the Lord says, "Ask, and it shall be given you; seek, [...] and it shall be opened unto you."

God loves us so much that He bought us back in His presence and paid the price just to keep us under His wing. Sometimes, we wonder what God sees in us. We are the apple of His eye. "For God so loved the world, that he gave his only Son, that whoever believes in him should not perish but have eternal life" (John 3:16, ESV). And when we can remember all this, we can say, "I surrender, Lord: everything is in Your hands; You are the God of Daniel, Isaac, and Moses; I depend on You for everything in my life." When you surrender yourself to Him, He will take over and give you the power and strength to go forward in life, and anything that comes up against you will never prosper.

How He Helps Us

Throughout this world, people come across things to be true. Take, for instance, science. It can tell us the different kinds of food to eat and drink that are okay. When it comes to the manifestation of the Lord, scientists cannot help you. When you and I come to understand that the Spirit in us is pleased, this gives us the ability and the opportunities to go forward in the Lord. If you and I resist these opportunities and pretend there is no God and live a life that could take us to the pit of hell, it is up to each of us. The very truth about this is the Spirit that God placed inside of us, which will transform and take you and me to the next level. The Spirit will let you know your true potential; no one on earth can give it to you. We must get it from God. Acts 2 states that on the day of Pentecost, the Holy Spirit came upon them. God did it for them, and He will do it for you. Trust in the name of the Lord.

There is one fruit with nine parts of the Holy Spirit that God imparts of His divine nature into the core of our personalities to help make us into a much better and holy people. Galatians 5:22-23 (KJV) says, "But the fruit of the spirit is love, joy, peace, longsuffering, gentleness, goodness, faith, meekness, temperance: against such there is no law." Peter said every human being can receive one of these gifts of the Holy Spirit if they repent and are baptized in the name of our Lord. You can be gifted too. This is the climax of what I am trying to say: it does not matter what limitations or circumstances you find yourself in; there is a God that can deliver you out of them.

God can turn things around. A member of your family may be sick; you may have lost your house; you may have been fired from your job; you may be going through some hard times. Whatever bad things you are experiencing in life, God can turn them around. Remember, when He took the Israelites out of Egypt, He told them, "I have a land for you; you must obey Me; if not..." Deuteronomy 28:64 (KJV) says,

> And the Lord shall scatter thee among all people; from the one end of the earth even unto the other; and there thou shalt serve other gods, which neither thou nor thy fathers have known, even wood and stone.

When you are at the end of your road, that is the time God can do His best work, that is the time when you can tell the enemy, "You may delay me, but you cannot stop me because He will send His angel to deliver me." "But the prince of the kingdom of Persia withstood me one and twenty days; but lo, Michael, one of the chief princes, came to help me; and I remained there with the kings of Persia" (Daniel 10:13, KJV). Also, in 1 Kings 17:1, Elijah, the prophet of the Lord, told wicked King Ahab that no rain would fall on the land of Israel during those years, except according to the word of the Lord. During all that time of drought, God took care of Elijah. Your assumption may be that this is only for some really special, really good people. You may come to some kind of conclusion that this kind of life either does not exist or exists only for a few people. There is a time in your life when God says no one can stop you; that was set from the beginning of the world.

He also hid Elijah by the brook Cherith and sent ravens to bring him food. Then, when the brook dried up, and there was no water for Elijah to drink, God sent him to Zarephath to the house of a poor widow, where He miraculously provided for Elijah. The widow and her young son were never out of food until God decided to send rain upon the land once more.

God's power and resources are not for special people at all. In fact, they cannot be earned by any human effort, ability, or goodness.

They can only be received as a free gift. They can only be accessed through humility, that is, by realizing we are just humans in need of our Creator. John 3:16 (KJV) says, "For God so loved the world, that he gave His only begotten Son, that whosoever believeth in him should not perish, but have everlasting life." Jesus said He stands at the door of our life and knocks, and if we let Him into our hearts and into our daily needs, He will lead us to life in all of its fullness.

Psalm 36:7 (ESV) states, "How precious is your steadfast love, o God! The children of mankind take refuge in the shadow of your wings." This is the attitude and position we should all have when we face the enemy and his attacks against us. Instead of listening to Satan telling us all the terrible things that are going to happen to us, we should start announcing to him all the good things God has planned for our lives and all the terrible things that are going to happen to Satan.

So that is the first step of how God will change things from negative to positive in a set time in your life. When God has established a set time in your life to accomplish His purpose, no one can change it. God wants to give you all the things you cannot provide for yourself. In order for you and I to receive all these things, we first must seek the face of the Lord. As we seek the face of the Lord, He will provide the way that we need to achieve all the things we desire. "But seek ye first the kingdom of God, and his righteousness; and all these things will be added to you" (Matthew 6:33, KJV).

Reading the Bible, the Word of God, will help you understand that when things go wrong, you can believe that there is a God that can help you. As you read, you can trust God because His time is different from man's time. He lifts kings up, and He puts kings down: all power is in His hands. Blessed is the name of the Lord. A set time was introduced to you because so many people take their own lives when things go wrong. We forget who controls time. The Word of God states there is a time coming when God will give you back everything that time took; He said there is a time come He will give you back everything that the locust, cankerworm, caterpillar, and the palmerworm have eaten (see Joel 2:25).

Choose Who You
Take Advice From

It was early in the morning when I ran into a good friend of mine. His name is Mike. He was angry because someone just gave him some advice that cut straight to his core, and he did not like it one bit. I told him it is important that we take on the characteristics of God in all circumstances. The Word of God tells us, "The LORD is righteous in all his ways, and holy in all His works" (Psalm 145:17, KJV).

Mike was in the process of buying a new taxi car to do some business, and he'd been working very hard putting all the money together. He wanted to be successful so badly he could feel it. Mike had always done well as a driver of a big taxi company but definitely had the talent and the ability to go out on his own. As Mike was in the process of borrowing some money from the bank, he decided to get some advice from a very good friend who had been in the business for a very long time. This was the guy who helped Mike, some years ago, to get a job in the company for which he now worked. Mike told his good friend all of his business plans and the dreams he had for the new company.

Mike expected his friend to agree with him. He was hoping for some good news, but instead, his friend responded, "I will tell you how I started my business, and it's my advice to you as well. I put together a group of people from my church, and we met every Monday and Friday evening. We asked the pastor to join us in prayer, and we took ourselves out of it and gave it to the Lord. That's how I built my company. It was not me. It was the Lord."

Mike did not want to hear that. All Mike wanted was for his business to go forward. Mike's reply to his friend's advice was, "These things are not the most important, not at the beginning." His friend told him that getting support from the Lord is very important if you want to be a successful businessman. Mike kept on pressing his friend for business secrets over and over, but his friend kept on telling him to surround himself with spiritual people who could pray.

As Mike spoke to me, he was mad. He told me how this guy had wasted his time, offering such useless advice. Mike didn't want to get close to spiritually wise people. He wanted to be successful. Mike started to complain. He wanted to start something to make money and accomplish his goals. One night after Mike and I spoke for hours in the morning, Mike called me, asking, "What does surrounding yourself with spiritual people have to do with driving a taxi?" I shared a scripture, Psalm 37:7 (KJV), with him: "Rest in the Lord, and wait patiently for him."

Mike ignored the advice he was given and started his taxi business. Within two years, he was breaking. He realized he could not start anything with his own knowledge. He thought his friend's advice would take too long. He could not see how being around some Christian people who like to pray could be the first and most important part of his strategy. Mike knew, for the most part, that God's way is the best way, but when he faced difficulties, he was tempted to question God's way and take shortcuts or invent what he thought was a better way. Mike's friend told him to consult the Lord in prayer, but he refused. Philippians 4:19 (KJV) says, "My God shall supply all your need according to his riches in glory by Jesus Christ."

Sometimes, our dissatisfaction with God's way comes as a result of envying the prosperity of unbelievers. As we are the children of God, it is important for us to remember we are in the world, but we are not of the world (John 17:16). God's way is the best way, and to stray from His way is to bring trouble upon ourselves. People who try to do it on their own rarely make it, and when they do, they usually cannot sustain the effort. There's also another reason that some do not find the way that God is making for them. It is so liberating to say, "Lord, I don't know what to do, and even if I did, I couldn't do it without You. But, Lord, my eyes are on You. I am going to wait and watch for You to do something about this situation because there is absolutely nothing I can do about it." Sometimes when we give God the situation, God will send people around us to help, but we reject them. Some of those people may not appear to be good, but God will use them in a way that you cannot imagine. Remember Joseph from the Bible and what his brothers did to him. They meant it for evil, but God turned it for good. God will use people, even those with bad intentions, to help you go further in life. Some of these people are not necessarily bad people. In fact, they can be some of our best friends and buddies. I think God makes them like that because we need them sometimes; they are crazy, funny, and full of love, and life cannot go on without them around. The Bible tells us about that kind of people in Deuteronomy 23:5 (KJV), where it states, "Nevertheless the LORD thy God would not hearken unto Balaam; but the LORD thy God turned the curse into a blessing unto thee, because the LORD thy God loved thee."

It is so hard to say you love certain people, but God admonishes us to show love to everyone. It is important that we acknowledge that there is something good and bad in everyone. However, some of the people we surround ourselves with are funny, but at the same time, we cannot depend on them for help because they are not focused on life. In reality, they are not helping you or me or the community; all they want is to do the things they enjoy.

These types of people like to play games and have fun all the time and avoid facing life's issues as they should, being grown-ups. These people avoid the deeper issues of life and are unable to help you move forward in life. Yes, it is easy to have fun with them, but they're not going to help us grow and find the love and beauty that

God promised us. You can have a friend around you night and day, but there is no positive movement to take you to the next level in life. At the same time, the things they want you to engage in will take you backward in life. My advice is to surround yourself with godly people who will pray with you and give you advice from the Word of God. People who will encourage you to seek His face before launching out into different endeavors.

Remember the Church

Bob was a man who had recently started to attend church, and that was good progress in his life. He was finding the new way that God had for him. When he went to see some friends after the Christmas holiday break, they looked at him differently. Bob was a little negative about a sickness he had. Some people said that they could see the energy and the growth that he had when he was going to church gone as if a light had been dimmed. He began to talk to people around him about the things he accomplished when he was going to church.

One lady said she felt sorry for him. It was as if a cloud had followed him into the room. What was also very apparent was that he did not seem to notice the aura surrounding him that others were seeing. He was just going about his life as if nothing was different, but he tried to ignore the fact that he was sick and in the hospital for a month. Bob was in denial about his sickness. He thought that it would go away in no time. The doctor told Bob, "Don't be afraid because it is a blood disease, and it is getting better."

Many people try to hide their sickness and try to work on it by themselves, and when they fail, they call for help. When they finally call for help, it is often too late. I think Bob was living in fear, whether in or out of the hospital. Consider what God said about fear. When we feel fear or begin to experience fearful thoughts, the very first thing we should do is pray. Mark 11:24 (KJV) says, "Therefore I say unto you, What things soever ye desire, when ye pray, believe that ye receive them, and ye shall have them."

I always say, "Pray about everything and fear nothing." We should set ourselves to seek God until we know we have the emotional and mental victory over the spirit of fear. As we seek God, we are focusing on Him instead of on our fears. We worship Him for who He is and express our appreciation to Him for the good He has done, is doing, and will continue to do. Bob wanted what God had for him, but unfortunately, just like a kid who thinks he doesn't need a teacher, he failed to take advantage of the gifted, loving, and wise people God put in his life.

The plan that God has for you and me is to put good people around us who are gifted to help us get where we need to go in life. Some of those people will show up in your life, sent by God at just the right time. Others you have to seek out on your own. Some will be professionals. Others may be neighbors or friends at work and church.

The Bible tells us when we love and support each other, we are actually doing the right thing that God Himself does. "Now about the gifts of the spirit, brothers and sisters, I do not want you to be uninformed" (1 Corinthians 12:1, NIV). Part of God's plans is to set a time in your life to surround you with good people whom He has gifted with the resources you need to get you where you need to go.

Here are some gifts that the good Lord promises us for us to help each other to go forward in this life:

The first gift is wisdom. God has His people on the earth who were given these gifts to help His people. Often, we do not possess all the wisdom and knowledge that we are going to need, so God speaks those things into our lives through wise people. And the Bible says trust in the Lord with all thine heart: and lean not unto thine own understanding (Proverbs 3:5 KJV).

Faith, defined as being sure of what we hope for and certain of what we do not see (see Hebrews 11:1). One of God's most powerful ways of working within a set time for us, His people, who can be role models for the world, Christ put His Holy Spirit in us. The Bible says, "We do not want you to become lazy, but to imitate those who through faith and patience inherit what has been promised" (Hebrews 6:12, NIV). Sometimes, when we are going through changes or trying to reach a goal, it's as if we're pushing our way uphill, but God said in His Word that He will never leave us or forsake us. Without God, we cannot live on this earth. Life experiences, such as overcoming illness, experiencing loss, or even reaching a dream, require faith.

Healing: God still performs miracles. God still heals people. Sickness, disease, pain, and death are still realities in this world, but in heaven, there will be no more pain, sickness, disease, suffering, or death. Living in this body, we will need healing; I pray night and day for God to send some people with the miraculous power to help us. What a blessing it is to have someone around us with the power of healing. I am talking about someone who understands the pain you are going through, someone who will intercede on your behalf in times of growth. "It shall come to pass, that before they call, I will answer; and while they are yet speaking, I will hear" (Isaiah 65:24, KJV).

THE LORD SENDS HELP

The Bible tells us when God calls someone, He equips that person in order for that person to get the job done in the right way. Gideon was fighting against the Midianites, so God told him that he has too many men. God want to get the glory, so he sends some of the men home. Because when they win, they will praise their self. God take a smaller number of men and win against the Midianites. Gideon doubted his own abilities but God will equips us with the Holy Spirit. Judges 7:14 (KJV) says, "And his fellow answered and said, this is nothing else save the sword of Gideon the son of Joash, a man of Israel: for into His hand hath God delivered Midian, and all the host."

God will always send someone to help you fight a battle or correct you when you are wrong. The Bible tells us that David slept with Bathsheba, Uriah's wife, and God sent Nathan to correct David. "The LORD sent Nathan to David. When he came to him, he said, 'There were two men in a certain town, one rich and the other poor'" (2 Samuel 12:1, NIV).

Moses was a man of God, but he took on too many responsibilities. Jethro, his father-in-law, gave him instructions to create the first government in Israel. Exodus 18:24 (KJV) says, "So Moses hearkened to the voice of his father in law and did all that he had said." Sometimes, it was a friend like Titus who encouraged the apostle Paul when he was depressed. Certainly, there are times when God supernaturally sends an angel, a vision, or even Jesus Himself to speak to someone. Watching television or listening to the radio, we hear about those things happening all over the world. But by and large, God's main program for us is to have loving and supportive friends who will be there to help us make it through whatever life decides to throw our way.

Life has its ups and downs, but today I am asking anyone out there, "What kind of plans do you have in this world?" Once a good friend of mine told me two is better than one because if two friends went up a hill and one fell, one would be there to help the other. When the night is cold and two people sleep together, it helps keep them warm. When two people live together, and one gets sick, the other one can take the sick one to the doctor.

Think back on your life. I am sure you can remember people who always encouraged you and people that wanted you to fail. There are some friends that will go the extra mile for you. They will help you and tell you about the love of God. These friends will confront you when you are headed for trouble. How many people can you depend on when all things break loose in your life, people to cry with, and when things get better, to laugh with you? On this journey of life, it is best to have good and godly people with you, so when the enemy comes upon you, there is someone to pray for you.

Here is a prayer for you to pray when life is not going well and everything seems to be going against you, and I can guarantee that the good Lord will show up to help you.

My God, my God, I am Your servant, and I cannot do anything on my own, so I am asking You to help me in this time of trouble. Remember when You told me that You will never leave me or forsake me? I am going through something that is bigger than me, so I am calling on You to help me on this journey of trouble. My God, You are an awesome God; You are the God of Daniel, Isaac, and Moses; You are the One who woke me up this morning. Psalm 57:1 (KJV) says, "Be merciful unto me, O God, be merciful unto me: for my soul trusteth in thee: yea, in the shadow of thy wings will I make my refuge, until these calamities be overpast." Thank You, Lord, for hearing my prayer.

You may look at this prayer and say it is too short. Yes, it is short, but remember, you are praying to God, not man. Look at the spiritual level of the prayer; God will answer it if it is coming from your heart.

When a pastor friend of mine stepped out to start his own church, he prayed night and day because it was hard work, but God was with him. I can remember when he was telling me that it was not easy for him to get people to help him. He said it was like taking out a tooth. I think he worked very hard. He pushed himself, and he is where God wants him. The challenge was great, but he made it. The same is true for all of us. If we stay focused on God and work hard, the way may seem tough, but we will be victorious in the end.

Thank God for the praying people in our lives who love and support us. Matthew 10:42 (KJV) says, "And whosoever shall give to drink unto one of these little ones a cup of cold water only in the name of a disciple, verily I say unto you, he shall in no wise lose his reward."

To my knowledge, there are two kinds of people in this world: those who pray to the true and living God and those that never pray. Thank God for the people that are praying because they are the ones keeping this world going. As a man of God, I am here to encourage you to keep up the good work because one day, the ones who are not praying will see your good work and start to pray. Some of those people will try to kill your dreams and turn you away from God's wonderful love. The ones that pray with you and help you are the ones that God put in your life to encourage you.

If they are still around, thank them and give them love. Tell them that you need them in order to make the next step in your journey. Ask them if they are available to you to support you in prayer. Some of them will be so glad for the invitation. Search your surroundings for good people who like to pray and ask who would like to help you build up God's church. Pray with them and ask God for His Holy Spirit to guide them. I prayed to God to send some people my way that believe in Him, so I can make a group go around the world and pray for people in need.

Use Judgment in
the Time of Trouble

Devon's wife found him in the basement slumped on the floor with a bottle of alcohol in his hand. She knew that he was an alcoholic for years, but she had no idea that it was that bad. Nor did anyone else in their family. Devon was a very successful man who had a lot of acquaintances. In a million years, no one would have guessed he was an alcoholic unless he had told them, and he was not about to tell anyone.

Drinking is one thing, but being an alcoholic is another. He often asked himself, "How can I tell my friends that I have sunk down so far? What will they think of me?"

Instead of worrying about what your friends will think, you should be asking, "What can they do to help me?" Devon felt as if he tried everything that he had always been taught to do to deal with alcohol. Devon read all the right books that were supposed to help people deal with alcohol; his mother was also giving him home medicine, and that did not work. He finally decided to attend Alcoholics Anonymous classes twice a week. At the same time, Devon did not want to burden a family member with his problems. He realized that no one could help him but God.

Devon's mother cried when she looked at her son; she asked the pastor to pray for her son. In about two weeks, God sent a good friend of the family. Her name is Barbara; she took Devon to a place actors and movie stars attended; it was expensive, but the doctors there were very good. The doctor interviewed him and was surprised by how low Devon was feeling. Devon sadly told the doctor, "I have no hope at all." In his mind, he thought nothing would ever change for him. He felt stuck in this problem with alcoholism, and no one understood. Devon asked the doctors, "Can you tell me how long all these procedures will take? The doctor answered Devon, "It will take some time, but with your patience, we will get you out of here as soon as possible."

Devon's wife spoke with the doctor; she said, "I am praying to God to help us put all of this behind." She also told the doctor, "The way Devon talks is bothering me. I have a feeling he wants to kill himself. The way he speaks seems like he thinks this problem will never get better."

One day, while I was talking with Devon, something came into my spirit, and at that time, I could see how far apart we were from each other. He was trying to give up, but that was the last thing on my mind. He had a negative feeling about his problem and started thinking about death, while I was certain that he would get well soon.

I spoke to Devon recently on the phone, and I told him, "I can see you getting better." He laughed at me and said, "I like your good spirit." The doctor told him that there was one more thing that he could try.

Psalm 16:1 (KJV) says, "Preserve me, O God: for in thee do I put my trust." Recovery would not be easy. I felt better when I heard those good words. God was working on behalf of Devon, and I can say there was hope even though he did not feel that way. Devon's wife shared with him, "My father was an alcoholic; I have experienced some bad things, and my family did not know what to do about it." Devon's wife tried to cheer him up.

The next morning, the doctor went to Devon's room and told him just from the little he had learned about him in the short time they spoke, "I know you can do it," but Devon refused to believe in himself.

Devon kept on complaining, "I don't want to be in this place." He kept on saying it. The doctor said, "I know, but you are." The

doctor told him, "We need to keep you here until you feel better."
Devon started to cry. Psalm 28:6 (KJV) says, "Blessed be the LORD,
because he hath heard the voice of my supplications."

"I don't want to be here," Devon protested much more adamantly,
"I will never get sober. Please let me go." The doctor replied, "Sorry,
I can't let you go. I am not accepting that. To my knowledge, I
believe you will get sober. I can understand how you feel right now.
You believe that there is no way out for you. It may look very hard
for you right now, but there is God; nothing is too hard for Him.
Right now, you cannot see it because He is working on the inside
of you." The doctor kept on telling him, "You just have to hang in
there with us and see for yourself."

The problem with alcoholics is that when you try to encourage
them to stop drinking, that does not have any effect on them. Many
people who abuse alcohol lose everything, including their family,
and some even end up living on the street. Devon went through a
lot, but God was with him. He received so much help. People from
all over donated things to him; one family paid half of his bill, some
people gave him clothes, and the list goes on. It is important to
know that you will go through things, but there is a time coming
when God said it is finished, and that is a set time—a time when
no one can stop you.

Knowledge Makes
the Difference

Many years ago, I was a driver for Elite Ambulance, and driving for that company, I had various experiences and learned a few valuable lessons. What I have learned came through a scenario that repeated itself and went like this: Someone who was a substance abuser or alcoholic came in the ambulance to be transported to the hospital. That person looked like someone without hope. Actually, that's an understatement given some of the situations that I have experienced. Some of them were struggling with crack cocaine, family abuse, and also alcoholism. Some lost their jobs or experienced long-term sexual abuse.

I had the opportunity to speak to some of those people. Most of them truly believed there was absolutely nothing that could make their situation better. Most of them gave up because of their condition. They believed there was no hope for them. But I am here to tell people struggling with various types of addictions and abuse that God is still caring for them; there is a time coming when God will say, "It is over" and "It is your time now." It is a set time of deliverance or redemption. A time when God will reveal His plans and purposes. That will be a set time in your life. Psalm 28:9 (KJV) says, "Save thy people, and bless thine inheritance: feed them also, and lift them up forever."

Working with these people helped me gain experience and understand things in a different way. When I looked into the matter, I found many people in such situations tend to give up, but I am here to let them know that I believe in God and there is hope for all. When God says it is over, it is over. When doctors say they cannot do anything about it, give the case to doctor God, and I guarantee He will fix it. What's the difference? In one phrase: There is nothing God cannot do. He is the One who made and healed many people. I am not trying to be a prophet or someone with special anointing, but I have experienced the power of God. I do know that there is nothing impossible for Him.

Some doctors have plans based on their experience with treating alcoholism; sometimes, the doctor's treatment plan works, and other times, it seems hopeless. The point I am making is this: Man's technology can only go so far, but when we put the situation to God, we will have hope, and we will see the benefits. "It is not you that shapes God, but God that shapes you. Since you are the work of God, await the hand of the artist who does all things in due season" (St. Irenaeus). Psalm 27:14 (KJV) says, "Wait on the LORD: be of good courage, and he shall strengthen thine heart: wait, I say, on the LORD."

Do Not Consume Alcohol

There are many different reasons that have been attributed to be possible causes of alcoholism and a variety of treatments. For example, an individual may drink to drown his or her problems, hoping the problem will go away. An individual may drink because he or she feels powerless, so the thought is, if the individual learns how to stop being manipulated, then the drinking will resolve itself. Likewise, if drinking is the result of unresolved grief or hurt and you resolve that pain, the thought is that the drinking gradually vanishes. If drinking stems from a biochemical problem and you take the right classes and therapy, you will see results. The next best thing to do is seek the face of the Lord in prayer and fasting and cry out to Him for help.

Regardless of the various schools of thought, one thing is sure: the knowledge doctors have regarding how to treat alcoholism was passed onto them by God. You must remember the only way you can get rid of this addiction is to submit yourself to God. God also warns us about the dangers of alcohol and drunkenness. He also says getting drunk causes you to lose control of yourself and do dangerous things that you wouldn't do if you were sober. Proverbs 23:31 (KJV) says, "Look not thou upon the wine when it is red, when it giveth his colour in the cup, when it moveth itself aright." My advice to you: Stay away from alcohol since it can be a difficult thing to control.

Many times, we feel helpless because we do not get the help we need. Sometimes, we add to the problem because we think that nothing can be done. Things indeed seem impossible. Sometimes, we have to change the way that we approach things and look at them from a different perspective.

In reality, in order for us to go forward, we have to depend on God. God has no limits when it comes to solving problems. He will tell us what to do and show us the way so that we can get the help we need as it applies to our situation.

The Bible helps us understand our situation and also gives us a clear look at how much God cares for us. James 2:1-5 (ESV) says,

> My brothers, show no partiality as you hold the faith in our Lord Jesus Christ, the Lord of glory. For if a man wearing a gold ring and fine clothing comes into your assembly, and a poor man in shabby clothing also comes in, and if you pay attention to the one who wears the fine clothing and say, "You sit here in a good place," while you say to the poor man, "You stand over there," or "Sit down at my feet," have you not then made distinctions among yourselves and become judges with evil thoughts? Listen, my beloved brothers, has not God chosen those who are poor in the world to be rich in faith and heirs of the kingdom, which he has promised to those who love him?

In this situation, God shows us an example of how some treat one type of people differently from another. The Bible tells us that God will use people that we look down on. Our task is to look to God for everything in our life because there is a time coming when the poor man will master over the rich man. Remember the story of Lazarus and the rich man (Luke 16:22). In this parable, Jesus discusses a rich man and a beggar. The rich man was unkind to the beggar. The time came when the beggar died, and angels carried him to Abraham's side. The rich man also died and was buried. The rich man ended up in hell, where he was in torment. He looked up and saw Abraham far away with Lazarus by his side.

People look at the outer appearance and judge others, but God looks at the inner appearance. "Consider it pure joy [...] when you encounter trials of many kinds because you know that the testing of your faith develops perseverance" (James 1:2, BSB). Without perseverance, you cannot finish the task that was put before you.

As I engaged in the Bible, I have learned that most of the people that God used greatly had to go through a transformation. There came a period in their lives when God seemed to hide them away while He worked on them and made changes in their character that would be necessary for their future assignment. God always has people put aside to carry out His assignment; when Elisha was afraid of the people who were killing the prophet, he complained to God he was the only prophet left. First Kings 19:18 (KJV) says, "Yet I have left me seven thousand in Israel, all the knees which have not bowed unto Baal, and every mouth which hath not kissed him."

Knowledge and Understanding Come from God

God gave His people knowledge and understanding. He says in His Word all things work together. Romans 8:28 (KJV) says, "And we know that all things work together for good to them that love God, to them who are the called according to his purpose." He also says in His Word any man lacking knowledge should ask. Proverbs 2:6 (KJV) says, "For the LORD giveth wisdom: out of his mouth cometh knowledge and understanding." Sometimes, when we are facing difficult tasks that we cannot take care of, we should call upon the Lord. He will give us the knowledge and understanding to go on.

Recently, I was talking to a lady whose husband was suffering from cancer. She said, "It's very hard for me, but I've learned something incredible. Each day comes with a new problem; I cry night and day over and over. Sometimes, I find myself totally not knowing what to do, but when I ask the Lord for help, He always tells me, 'Read My Word.' I pray and ask the Lord one way or another; the answer I need will be just right on time."

I can understand God is never late; He is always on time. He is an on-time God. Remember the death of Lazarus. It took Jesus some time to get to Lazarus, and although the situation seemed hopeless, Lazarus was resurrected. John 11:11 (KJV) says, "These things said he: and after that he saith unto them, [...] but I go, that I may awake him out of sleep." This lady understood that God would, at the right time, give her the knowledge to face the problems she was experiencing.

God Will Send People
with Understanding

There are many situations you and I do not understand, but God will send us help. Some of these situations are very serious and can create big problems. In reality, there is someone who can resolve our problems, but first, we must pray for help. Second, we must seek people who experience the same struggles that we are going through. When my wife and I were facing problems with bills, and the money was not enough, I left it in her hands. She is an accountant and knows how to move money around. The fact is we do not have all the answers, but God will send people our way who understand the problem.

When Samuel and Rachel were trying to refinance their house, it was so hard. Because of a previous claim they filed to repair the roof, the bank refused to refinance their house; the couple tried more than one bank, and the answer was no. After one year, the couple could not get a breakthrough. One Sunday morning, Samuel was walking in the church building when the pastor came out of his car. Samuel saw him and turned back, saying, "I would like to talk to you." The pastor said, "Make it quick because I am late." Samuel discussed their problem with the pastor. He said, "I will talk to Brother Brown about your problem; he is a bank manager."

Samuel and Rachel prayed and fasted for two weeks. One morning, while the couple was getting ready to go to work, the phone rang. The person on the next end was Brother Brown, who asked them, "Can you come into my office today?" The couple said yes and hung up the phone; they started to praise God, kissing each other and crying. They went to the bank: everything went pretty well.

Sometimes, when we have a problem, we intend to look all over the world for help, and help is right in your backyard. God will take care of His people. He made a promise to us; He will never leave you or forsake you.

SEEK STRUCTURED KNOWLEDGE

Robert made a phone call to a family member every weekend, but he knew that would never give him the knowledge he needed. He prayed to God to send someone specific who would understand his problem. He emphasized the word "specific," meaning someone who was skilled in the form of help he needed.

For instance, dealing with a father or mother who drinks and smokes is a good example of a challenging situation that requires a specific type of help. All those habits are very serious and most often require someone with psychological training to help. Many times, some family members call emergency vehicles for their loved ones who are caught up in an addiction. Some people try to deal with it themselves or attend mutual support groups, and nothing works. When some doctors hear that the family has not sought the appropriate help, they become frustrated.

They find themselves almost screaming at them to get in contact with a specific behavioral therapist who has dealt with hundreds of alcoholics or smoking addicts. Some behavioral therapists without that experience do not know what to do with an addict. The help that addicts need almost always has to come from a structured substance abuse program.

There are many programs around that can help us in the areas that we are struggling. We can find help by listening to advertisements; there is some sort of help available if we look. There are so many programs out there that can help us, such as support for grief, National Institute on Alcohol Abuse support groups, recovery programs, counselors, and the list goes on. Stop being hard on yourself.

It breaks my heart to see people refuse to go forward in life and seek knowledge and help when it's so widely available! And today, cost does not have to be an obstacle because there are many fine, affordable programs available in different organizations.

The Power of Prayer

In my Sunday school class, we talked about prayer and the need for it; we discussed how we should get active in seeking God in prayer because there is a time coming when we may not be able to pray. Prayer that goes to God from a good heart, is based on the right motives, and is not selfish, will be answered by Him (Jeremiah 29:12). "Therefore I tell you, whatever you ask for in prayer, believe that you have received it, and it will be yours" (Mark 11:24, NIV).

I can remember when I used to deliver food for a company whose name I am not permitted to say. I used to pray for most of them. One lady said that when we all prayed for her, God answered her prayers and her husband said God is good. She was not praying for long life; she just needed some help with a special type of bed and some medications. There are many testimonies about prayer. Some people do not believe that prayer works. When you are a child of the Most High God, prayer is the way to communicate with Him. I dedicate my life to prayer. If it was not for prayer, where would I be today? I can remember when the enemy came upon me; prayer was my food and my sleep. In the book of Esther, when Haman was about to kill Mordecai, Queen Esther told all the Jews to fast and pray for three days (Esther 4:16). Prayer can change things. All we must do is believe in it and know that God ordained prayer for us to get us to the next part of life.

Prayer is like having a farm; you plant a kernel of corn. The corn starts to grow right in front of you, but you cannot see that the corn is growing because it is growing out of sight. In the same way, when you pray, the prayer is taking effect in your life, but you may not see it right away. You will know with confidence that God can hear you when you pray. It is very important for you to open that line of communication. Praying, knowing that no matter how far you are , your connection with Him can never be lost. Ephesians 6:18 (KJV) says, "Praying always with all prayer and supplication in the Spirit, and watching thereunto with all perseverance and supplication for all saints."

When we as people in this flesh sinned and deserved God's judgment, God the Father sent His only Son to satisfy that judgment for those who believed in Him. Jesus set an example for us on how to pray. He prayed for His disciples and for every generation to come that would follow Him. Jesus's prayer was that God would protect and strengthen them as long as they were in this world. He also prayed for those who would come to believe in Him through the gospel message. (Matthew 6:9 KJV) say after this manner therefore pray ye: our father which art in heaven, hallowed be thy name. As we follow Christ's example, we, too, must freely give ourselves to prayer. Some people look on prayer has an unselfish work that is often unseen and unappreciated by others. Some people do not like to pray, but they like to experience the resolved when you and I pray. As a prayer warrior, I am not seeking to be seen by man but rather to stand in the presence and pleasure of the Lord (Matthew 6:5; Hebrews 7:25). Our times with God the Father bring us into the oneness of the lost for the kingdom and help us demonstrate His compassion for the hurting and His love for others, even our enemies.

Anyone who wants to move the heart of God must come to Him in prayer in a humble manner. When we humble ourselves before God in true repentance, God can move on our behalf. When Hezekiah was about to die, he prayed. Isaiah 38:5 (KJV) says, "Go, and say to Hezekiah Thus said the LORD, the God of David thy father, I have heard thy prayer, I have seen thy tears: behold, I will add unto thy days fifteen years."

Just like many of us, the apostle Paul said he did not cease giving thanks for others while making mention of them in his prayers (Ephesians 1:16) Philippians 1:3-4). Paul, like Jesus, believed God. As a result, prison gates were opened, souls were saved, the afflicted were healed, and lives were transformed. Prayer is powerful, especially when it is based upon God's Word.

I can guarantee you this: If you spend more time talking with the Father and reading His Word, your prayer will begin to reflect the heart, mind, and Word of the Lord. God's Word never changes. It is the same yesterday, today, and forever. God will meet you right where you are, using the amount of knowledge you have. A pastor friend of mine told me a story. He said that he visited the doctor for a physical, and he took all the recommended tests. After two weeks, the doctor called him and told him he had prostate cancer. He was so devastated he did not know what to do. The following week he attended church and asked all the members to pray for him. He made the appointment for the surgery, and the surgery was successful. My pastor friend has lived to see the age of eighty. Some people like to hide their sickness, so no one knows that they need to pray a specific, targeted prayer. James 5:14 (KJV) says, "Is any sick among you? Let him call for the elders of the church; and let them pray over him, anointing him with oil in the name of the Lord."

Ask God for the knowledge on how to deal with your sickness. Sometimes, we have to ask God to give us a verse that applies to the situation for which we are praying and pray it. For example, you might pray Colossians 1 by inserting your own name or the name of your family and friends, asking that you

> may be filled with the knowledge of His will in all spiritual wisdom and understanding, so that you will walk in a manner worthy of the Lord, to please him in all respects, bearing fruit in every good work and increasing in the knowledge of God; strength-

ened with all power, according to His glorious might, for the attaining of all steadfastness and patience; joyously giving thanks to the Father, who has qualified us to share in the inheritance of the saints in light.

Colossians 1:9-12 (NASB)

Praying your prayer this way will cause God's Word to come alive in your heart and soul. Praying God's Word brings out the truth and gives you the answer that you are looking for. God Himself said that His Word will not return to Him empty without accomplishing what He desires and without succeeding in the matter for which He sent it (Isaiah 55:11). When you pray the Word, however, it must be quickened by the Holy Spirit so you may speak forth with anointing.

When you pray, avoid religious activity. Pray the Word based on faith, believing that you are in agreement with God's will for the circumstance. Let faith and the Spirit be the motivation behind your prayer. Then, God will take you to the next level in your life, and you can have the assurance that He will work in your favor.

The Bible tells us that without faith, it is impossible to please God, for he who comes to Him must believe that He is and that He is a rewarder of those who seek Him (Hebrews 11:6). When you pray, it must be based on faith, and it will bear fruit for the kingdom and please God. When you pray, it is a privilege and honor to have communication with God in faith. You will speak to Him, and He will answer you and give you the direction, wisdom, knowledge, and strength to go on in this life.

Remember Where God Brought You From

Dennis was excited about his new job, as excited as his family had ever seen anyone. His new position was with the marketing department of a family-owned company that sold car parts. He was hired to build relationships with car dealers, some mechanic shops, and other key influencers in the car industry that the sales force could follow up on.

In the first few weeks, he thought the course of his whole life had changed. Talented and bright, Dennis had always thought that he could be a success. He was extremely well-liked, and with his brains and personality, he seemed like a shoo-in for any job that required creativity, intelligence, and people skills. Yet, it hadn't happened. The truth was, at forty, he wasn't much further along than he'd been in his late twenties. But this job, he assured me, was going to change his life.

He could not believe how perfectly suited he was for the position. His first assignment was to take a group of car dealers to play golf, befriend them for a couple of days while they were in town. "Can you believe it?" he asked his wife. He continued to tell her about how well it went, how he kept them all laughing, and how he knew that the sales group was going to score big with them because of what he had done. He could just see the future forming right in front of him—a corner office and people coming to see him.

Dennis continued with some other meetings and what had always been true: people loved him. Things looked bright. Then, one day, about the fourth week, he got a call from the boss's office reminding him that he hadn't turned in his paper works or expense report. "My mistake," Dennis apologized, "Sorry. I got held up with a new dealer. The boss is working on a new thing. They have me running all over the place. I'll get what you need at your office later today." He hung up the phone and went right back to what he was doing and forgot about what he was supposed to do. He kept on doing different things and forgot all about the promise he had made. This was a familiar pattern with Dennis, so later, he did not come. Next time, when the phone rang, the boss himself said, "Hi, Dennis. I just received a call from Peter, the CFO. He said you were supposed to send some paperwork. They're waiting on the paperwork from you; it is holding them up. I would appreciate it if you could send it to them in order for them to finish the analysis. What's the deal? Why aren't you sending them those papers?" "Sorry," Dennis apologized, "I will send all my paperwork over to them right away."

"Thank you. It doesn't look professional when those guys keep on calling me about paperwork," the boss responded. "This is not good for me since I'm trying to get our budget increased. In the future, I would appreciate it if you submitted your papers on time." "Sorry, boss. It won't happen again," Dennis reassured him. *Something is wrong*, Dennis thought as he placed the phone down. *That seemed a little heavy-handed*, he thought as he looked off into space, *I am tired of the harassment over a bunch of paperwork. I wish they would understand what I am doing is for the company.* He even felt a little upset and underappreciated.

A week later, Dennis was to submit an important research report to the top management for the annual meeting of the board of directors. The same thing happened. He forgot to submit the paperwork on time, and once again, his boss was on the phone. He was not pleased with what was going on with Dennis, "Where is the information? The board needs it for the meeting." Again, Dennis said, "Sorry, boss. The presentation meeting at the car company yesterday used up my time. But I will start on it right away." Dennis explained.

The boss was concerned about what seemed to be an emerging pattern with Dennis, so one day, he decided to have a meeting with him. Dennis needed to know that each time he delayed submitting paperwork, he created problems for the rest of the staff, and the boss would appreciate it if Dennis could do better. The boss appreciated the good work that Dennis was doing, but his irresponsibility in turning in necessary information was getting in the way. The boss knew that, even with all the people skills in the world, paperwork is your first priority, especially when working for a big company. He also wanted to get off on the right foot with Dennis. The boss liked him and was really impressed with his intelligence and relational strength.

There was a problem at the meeting. The boss thought the meeting was going to be a constructive give and take, but it turned into a train-wreck situation. Dennis's reaction was outrageous. He tried to defend himself, "Why does everyone seem to look on me as a bad person when I'm doing such a great job in this company? This is like having a nightmare," Dennis griped. The boss just listened.

Dennis continued, "I am hurt by your negative talk and trying to put me down."

"You are taking it the wrong way," the boss responded gently but with authority. "This is very important to all of us to reach our goal. It is not personal. You are doing a fantastic job. This is about your priorities and taking your job more seriously."

The boss left the meeting and hoped that Dennis could understand where he was coming from. As a seasoned manager with a lot of experience, he had remained firm and had not allowed Dennis's reaction to get in the way of what he was supposed to do. The way Dennis behaved caused the boss to make a prediction: Dennis was walking on thin ice. It was about two weeks later when the prediction came true. As Dennis got more information and input, he resisted more and started to say bad things about the boss and other managing teams. Dennis forgot where he was coming from. He griped about the management to his peers, and that caused even more trouble for him. It came to a point when Dennis's poor administrative performance, as well as his divisiveness, could not be overlooked regardless of his talents and contribution. He showed no appreciation to all the managers who had such great hopes for him; he was terminated.

Because of the way Dennis reacted to things, his boss knew that it was coming soon. The next day, he announced to the team that they would never see him again, nor would Dennis's character issues affect them. It was so sad that Dennis's problem would continue to plague his wife and children through two more jobs and disappointments. Dennis's family had to move and start over two more times until Dennis finally came to the conclusion that he needed to change and remembered where God brought him from. Just like the children of Israel, who God took out of Egypt, but who refused to listen to Him, they forgot where God took them from. Deuteronomy 26:8 (KJV) says, "And the LORD brought us forth out of Egypt with a mighty hand, and with an outstretched arm, and with great terribleness, and with wonders."

THE POWER OF PRIDE

There is something inside of us called "pride." Here is how it works.

We all have relationships, experiences, and lessons in life that are sometimes painful, difficult, and, for whatever reason, hard to process. As a result, we walk around with certain feelings, patterns, and conflicts that do not really relate to the present but to people and events from a previous time. Because of all those things, a door was open, and pride stepped inside, and it got in the way of present situations, present relationships, or present goals. And the sad thing about that is when you do not remember where you were and who helped you, you still walk around like everything is okay, but pride will never go away until it is dealt with.

What happened with Dennis was not new at all. It was an old pattern in his life that was reenacted one more time around a new goal in a new place with new people. For Dennis, it was all about his relationship with his mother. Dennis never knew his father, so Dennis's mom has been a strong, overbearing lady. Dennis felt he could never please her. It seemed that no matter what Dennis did, he was not quite good enough for his mother. He always felt put down and unappreciated. He would try his best to please his mom but to no avail. Colossians 3:23 (KJV) says, "And whatsoever ye do, do it heartily as to the Lord and not unto men."

As a result, Dennis was deeply hurt and developed a sensitivity to criticism for a good reason. In many ways, his mom was just mean. So, Dennis felt bad about himself in comparison to others. As he grew older, he did what most of us do: he worked hard to overcome those feelings. He performed well and tried hard. And because he was very talented, he often did well until some significant authority figure like his previous boss started to criticize him in some way. Then, he would characteristically feel bad about himself, not good enough, unappreciated, and hurt. When Dennis remembered all the things he had been through in his relationship with his mother, he would feel those same emotions in present-day relationships with authority figures whom he wanted to please. Trying to overcome his feelings had not worked because Dennis had never dealt with his feelings and patterns from the past. He tried to hide these feelings and patterns, but they continued to be present and active inside him. The chance would come again and again for those feelings to be expressed, like in a relationship with a new authority figure. He would feel hurt and begin to resist the things that his boss would ask of him. He refused to follow directions, and at the same time, they would criticize him. All of those things added up, and eventually, he would lose his job.

Dennis's behavioral patterns were not the best, but at the same time, his bosses generally did not intend to put him down. Over the years, he has been carrying this baggage of guilt, sensitivity, and hurt that has never been dealt with. Sometimes, his personality would seem like that of a child. His behavior caused people to think that they were dealing with a child, and not many companies like to employ children. This mentality caused him to lose his job and his family. His ways of doing things for the company were okay, but when it was time for him to present paperwork, he ignored it and did not try to fulfill his boss's expectations.

Dennis must go back to the Bible as in 1 Corinthians 13:11 (KJV), it says, "When I was a child, I Spake as a child, I understood as a child I thought as a child: but when I became a man, I put away childish things." He has to learn how to respect authority and be a man. Dennis has to learn if hurtful things have happened to him in the past and he has not yet dealt with them, those old events will come back and build a wall around his heart and cause problems. Dennis was hurt in the past, and it was affecting him. He refused to take correction from his boss; he felt as if he were being picked on. He remembered the things he had gone through with his mother and thought the world was against him. Psalm 27:10 (KJV) says, "When my father and my mother forsake me then, the LORD will take me up."

Break Down the Walls
around Your Life

What do I mean when I say God has a set time for you and me, and no one can change it? Here is some miraculous encouragement to elevate your spirit from Nehemiah 2:3. The Bible told us about Nehemiah, who was a cupbearer for the king. He heard about the destruction of the wall in Jerusalem. He was so sad. One day, he asked the king to give him the opportunity to go back and rebuild Jerusalem. The king said yes and gave him a letter to pass beyond the river. He also retrievem material to help rebuild the city. The favor of the Lord was on Nehemiah: God's work must be done; God will use men and women from different generations.

When it comes to the work of the Lord, it is a set time, a time that no one can change; the wall was broken down for years, but the time has come to rebuild it. As it is in the spiritual, so it is in the natural. God set a time for what you are going through and can change things around. John 11:17 told us about the death of Lazarus. When Mary and her sister Martha sent and called Jesus, He took a long time to come because it was not yet the time to raise Lazarus. There was a set time to raise Lazarus. Jesus delayed for two days, and when Jesus got there, he was in the grave for four days. With the power of the Lord, Jesus Christ set a time in our life to do things. We, as human beings, try to change God's plan sometimes and put ourselves into problems. Christians should take the Word of the Lord in their life, and they will achieve the things that God promised them. Sometimes, when we pray our prayer, it is not answered at the same time: the Lord is waiting for the right time to answer our prayer. I can remember when my wife first moved to Georgia, she was seeking employment. She sent out many resumes; she also went on some interviews and was promised to call soon. She never received a phone call; one day, a friend told her about a part-time position on her job, and she accepted the offer. She was working for one year, and the company laid her off. On her way home, she made a call back to the previous job. The boss said, "I am sorry. Are you still interested in the job? Come to work tomorrow."

God has a set time for your life, and no one can change it.

Living with Cancer

Many people are living today because of the mercy of God. Yet, no problem can be overcome until you and I admit that it exists.

In 2006, a friend of mine, Michael, was diagnosed with cancer. He was so sick he had to stay in bed all the time. He refused to give up the fight with this sickness. He was not a church member. When he first came to this country, he stayed with me for one year, and he saw me attend church on a regular basis. I tried to encourage him to come to church with me, but it never happened. Unfortunately, he went to live with his girlfriend in a different state. About two years later, a mutual friend called me to inform me about his sickness. I was so surprised. The Bible told us in Ephesians 5:17 (KJV), "Wherefore be ye not unwise, but understanding what the will of the Lord is."

My wife and I went on to pay him a visit. Tears came from my eyes when I saw him. I can remember in the Bible when Jesus visited Lazarus, and He wept. He did not weep because of the death of Lazarus; He wept, seeing how sin had taken over human beings. This young man got the opportunity to give his life to the Lord, and he refused to do so. My wife and I prayed with him. The next week, we went to visit him. As soon as we entered the room, he turned to me and said, "I was trying to call you because I would like to go to church with you." I looked at my wife, and she looked back at me. Then I said to myself, "How can we do this? He is in no condition to walk. The only way for him to visit a church is to take him on a bed."

I am sharing this story with my readers to encourage them to go to church and give their life to the Lord whenever they get the opportunity. You may never get a second chance, so I encourage you to break down the walls around your life and let God in. Sometimes, those walls can be a boyfriend, girlfriend, family member, brother, sister, or boss. You have to get rid of them in order for you to get to the next level in life.

In order for you and I to receive the plan that God has for us, we must first repent. It is so easy to call upon the Lord when sickness is in your body and walking is a challenge, but I encourage you to serve the Lord right now. The love of the Lord will help you through your sickness. Remember when Hezekiah got sick, and he prayed to the Lord to give him fifteen more years on his life, and he received them? If you and I stay with the Lord, we can talk with Him, and He will give us the same privilege. Second Kings 20:3 (KJV) says, "I beseech thee, O LORD, remember now how I have walked before thee in truth and with a perfect heart, and have done that which is good in thy sight. And Hezekiah wept sore."

Michael had friends and loving people around him to support him, but what he needed was the spirit of the Lord in him to heal him. When you and I stay under the umbrella of the Lord and have a history with Him, we can ask Him anything, and He will answer us. God's process of healing us is to give us free will. It is up to us to follow Him, and if we choose to follow Him, we are under the umbrella of protection. When the enemy comes upon us, God is right there for us. Michael's pride was stopping him. He worried about what his friends would say, but he forgot about the love of God. God will give him the love that people from his past never gave to him.

Then, you would be able to see that there is a living God who can heal and restore your heart. The next step is to receive the care and healing you need to deal with whatever sickness you are experiencing. If individuals in the church become sick, they have to allow others to give them godly care and love to help them get back on their feet. Remember the Bible says, "Is any sick among you? let him call for the elders of the church; and let them pray over him, anointing him with oil in the name of the Lord" (James 5:14, KJV).

Michael, likewise, needed someone to tell him about the goodness of God and what God could do for him. Be honest with yourself. Many times, we forget how God has taken us out of some bad situations. If we feel guilty or ashamed of the way we treat God and the things we have done to Him, it may be difficult for us to have a relationship with Him. We can change all those negative feelings and live a life that is pleasing to God. We must be free from the guilt and shame associated with previous failures and shortcomings. Leaving things that we used to do behind us means that we know that God totally accepted us.

When did God totally accept you? There are some things that you have to do to make that transformation. Remember that there is only one true living God, and He sent His Son to die for us. He will forgive us and love us. All we have to do is communicate with Him and do His will. The Lord makes promises that He will never leave us or forsake us. He will take all of our sins and put them in the sea of forgetfulness.

> Thanks be to God, who always leads us in triumph in Christ, and manifests through us reveals the fragrance of the knowledge of Him in every place. For we are a fragrance of Christ to God among those who are being saved and among those who are perishing.

> 2 Corinthians 2:14-15 (NASB)

To be a fragrance of Christ, first, you have to be clean and set free from the guilt and shame of your past. God will set a time in your life to elevate you to the next level. First, you have to have confidence in Him that "if we ask any thing according to his will, he heareth us: And if we know that he hear us, whatsoever we ask, we know that we have the petitions that we desired of him" (1 John

5:14-15, KJV). The Bible told us that whatever we ask of the Lord, He will make available for everyone who wants it. All we have to do is accept that He went on the cross and died for you and me. We got a second chance in life, so we no longer have to look back on the things we have done because He already paid the price for you and me. "He was wounded for our transgressions, he was bruised for our iniquities: the chastisement of our peace was upon him; and with his stripes we are healed" (Isaiah 53:5, KJV). If you think that God can help you, pray and ask Him for help because there is nothing that is impossible, that He cannot do. He makes a way when there is no way for all of us to get a fresh start, and He does so each and every day. Sometimes we fail, but if we ask for His help, He is always there for us. Some people think that they are so deep in sin that no one can help them, but His grace and mercy are good enough for them.

When you confess your sins, it is good for your soul. The Lord starts to live inside of you and forgives you; then, you start to forgive others. Matthew 6:12 (KJV) says, "And forgive us our debts, as we forgive our debtors." The human mind is so complex. Whenever we sin or fail, we tend to think that others will not accept us, so we feel isolated and alone. Sometimes, God forgives us, but we persist in sins, so God allows us to experience difficulties or burdens to put us to the test. The word "burden" here literally means hardship "that which he has given you," or the word may simply mean "problem." Did you ever think of your burden as a gift from God? To understand this is to take the first step in the transformation of trouble. That trial, disappointment, loss—is that God's doing? Yes, He has permitted it.

He has trusted you with it for some very wise and loving purpose (Romans 8:28). It has not come because of "fate" or "bad luck." It may have come from the devil, but only with the Lord's full permission. Therefore, accept it from His hands. One reason God allows us to bear burdens is that they may bring us closer to Him (Romans 8:19). It is easy to forget God and become slack when things go smoothly, when there are no challenges. Psalm 119:71 (KJV) says,

"It is good for me that I have been afflicted; that I might learn thy statutes." Every Christian should cast their burden upon the Lord. He is the waymaker; here, we see a further reason why the Lord gives us these burdens: that in our weakness, we may prove His strength and the all-sufficiency of His grace. God wants us to learn that when problems come our way, we know His status.

Leave the burden with the Lord. Once we have cast our burden upon Him, He assumes full responsibility for it and for us, and He promises to sustain or uphold us. How wonderful this is: He will sustain you; He will never let the righteous fall. Never? No, never. Psalm 55:22 (KJV) states, "Cast thy burden upon the LORD, and he will sustain thee; he shall never suffer the righteous to be moved."

Look into Yourself

Kevin and Melisa are two young people that work in the same office. They both take a lunch break at the same time. One day, the supervisor asked Melisa, "Why are you taking lunch at the same time with Kevin? She replied, "Because he is a man with pride." If you talk to Kevin about his pride, you will find out that he is carrying a lot of resentment in his heart. He talks about the things that people have done to him. But looking back at his employment history can help you determine the type of person he is. He had a real problem letting go of the ways he felt others had let him down. Because of the resentment in his heart and the lack of forgiveness, Kevin thinks the world is against him. In his mind, he thinks that everyone who has ever hurt him is still hurting him every day. He keeps on talking about things that happened a long time ago; these are alive in his memory, and those memories are eating away at his soul. He is trying to forget the past but is still carrying that pride into each new situation that he engages in, and the result is not good. The way he portrays himself reflects his self; he is suspicious toward new authority and is somewhat of a ticking time bomb.

Take a look at this kind of spiritual bacteria at work. There are some things that we must let go of because if we keep them inside, they will eat us up. We should try to live the life of God. The Bible tells us that God remembers our sins no more. He lets things go. He pardons us. He does not hold anything against us. And as a result, He cleans your mind from everything that everyone ever does to you in your life and gives you a fresh start. Once God said it is over, it's over. An old saying goes like this: "You are free to love again." God hears your cry, and He sees your tears, forgives you, and takes you back. All of us have fallen short, and God understands that. God provided a way for us to be free of the burdens we are carrying in our hearts. He reminds us that He forgives you and me of our sins, so we must forgive others that sinned against us. When we forgive others, we are free.

When you forgive others, do not feel like you are the weaker person. Forgiveness is a positive work with the Lord. We forgive others when we let go of resentment and give up any claim to be compensated for the hurt or loss we suffered. The Bible teaches that unselfish love is the basis for true forgiveness since "doth not behave itself unseemly seeketh not her own, is not easily provoked, thinketh no evil" (1 Corinthians 13:5, KJV As a child of the Highest God, we must know it is very important to forgive others. As long as we feel like someone owes us, we're tied to him or her by the offense committed. But the good book uses the word "forgive," which means "to cancel a debt." We must take into consideration when we forgive that person, he or she no longer owes us, and we have to release that person. As soon as that person pays the debt, we must forgive him or her, and the person is no longer obligated to us. When you refuse to forgive someone, you break your full communication with the Lord. It can desensitize you to spiritual things. When you ask forgiveness for yourself and those who have sinned against you, you will be set free and able to wake in the right relationship with God and man. Forgiveness also frees the other person or changes the circumstances that are causing the problem. It allows the Holy Spirit to do His job, which is to bring conviction about the sin so righteousness can be restored.

If you are having a problem forgiving someone, determine to obey God's Word and refuse to be guided by your feelings. Do not let pride keep you from having the right relationship with God. Lay down your hurts, self-righteous attitude, and hostilities. Forgive the person who has wronged you, no matter how unjust the offense may be. You will then experience a release in your spirit, and your feelings will begin to follow. Your fellowship with the Lord will then be restored. The Word of God says,

> For if you forgive other people for their offenses, your heavenly Father will also forgive you. But if you do not forgive other people, then your father will not forgive your offenses.

Matthew 6:14-15 (NASB)

I have discovered that most people find it fairly easy to forgive others, very difficult to serve God, and almost impossible to forgive themselves. Total forgiveness, however, is essential to your effective praying life.

Pray to the Lord to help you make a decision every morning that you will wake in forgiveness throughout the day. Stay strong. Do not wait until you get into a confrontation and then try to forgive the next person who has wronged you. Have your mind set and choose to forgive others as God has forgiven you and do it at the time of the offense, just as Jesus did in(Luke 23:34KJV).say then said Jesus, father forgive them; for they know not what they do. Remember, forgiveness itself is not enough: you must also repent. To repent is to feel such regret or remorse that you turn away from your thoughts or actions and release others from any bondage you or they hold. Unless this is done, you will never be free. Forgiveness and repentance go hand in hand (Proverbs 28:13KJV) say" he that cover his sins shall not prosper: but whoso confesses and forsakes them shall have mercy". (Matthew 3:6 KJV). say and were baptized of him in Jorden, confessing their sins. When some people say that they forgive, but they are still holding on to the wrong attitudes, they rebel against God.

The Bible tells us that when someone does you something wrong, it is not good for you to get back to that person. I can remember working at a big company, and my coworker was telling lies about me. He told the boss that he saw me drinking alcohol, though I never take pleasure in drinking or smoking. This young man had some problems in his life, so when I came home, I prayed for him, telling God to help him. Sometimes, when someone says bad things about you, that person cannot help himself because the evil one has control over that person. Matthew 16:23 (KJV) says, "But he turned, and said unto Peter, Get thee behind me, Satan: thou art an offence unto me: for thou savourest not the things that be of God, but those that be of man." Jesus was not calling Peter Satan; Jesus knew those thoughts were not coming from Peter. Jesus was getting ready to go on the cross, and Peter rebuked him, but if Jesus did not go on the cross, where would you and I be today? When God the Father saw the sins of the world, He sent His Son to die for His children because He loves us so much. John 3:16 (KJV) says, "For God so loved the world, that he gave his only begotten Son, that whosoever believeth in him should not perish but have everlasting life." In one word: the apostle Paul told us that the reason why Jesus went on the cross to bring us back to God was because we were so far away from Him. Jesus did not die for one nation; He died for the world. Second Corinthians 5:21 KJV) says, "For He hath made him to be sin for us, who know no sin; that we might be made the righteousness of God in Him." When I was just visiting a church, I was not a Christian; the preacher sermon was Jesus on the cross. On my way home, my spirit was troubled: it was hard for me to get it how one man could die for the world. When the Lord saved me and I started to study the Bible, I came up on 1 Corinthians 2:14 (KJV) that says, "But the natural man receiveth not the things of the Spirit of God: for they are foolishness unto him: neither can he know them because they are spiritually discerned." My advice to everyone who does not know the true and living God: pray and ask Him to save you from all the bad things in this world. His plan is for us not to go to hell. He loves us; your prayer will be answered, and He will save you.

Examine Your Path

Sometimes, we are hurt, and our pride takes us into the atmosphere of unforgiveness, and we do the same things over and over like a pattern, but we never learn from those hurtful situations. As a young boy, Dennis learned that authority, any authority, was unreasonable and impossible to please and that he was powerless to do much in that kind of relationship. He found a way and developed a strategy to deal with his mother. He tried passively to avoid her and resisted doing what was asked of him. Dennis avoided talking to his mother directly about their problem but would go behind her back to find solace and comfort. He never learned how to solve the problem and move on with his life. He overlooked things, and that was why a late expense report, which was a small oversight, could grow to be something that could end his career.

The way that you pattern your life and deal with people and your relationship with others have a great impact on you. You think you know how to operate and negotiate those issues in a certain environment where God's Word was never practiced. Perhaps those dysfunctional aspects in your life are holding you back from all that He would like for you to have right now. The Lord has been in the business for a long time, helping people out of their problems.

He emancipated His people out of slavery in Egypt and then gave them new ways of dealing with life. He took them out and made them into a nation and told them to turn from the ways of their father, previous generations. He told them, "If you obey Me, I will bless you, but if you disobey Me, I will put you in the four parts of the world." It's time to obey the Lord because you cannot do things on your own. When you try to do things on your own, it comes out badly, so give God a chance. Change your ways of doing things and help someone along the way of life because God is with you. When we visit the store, we should buy enough so we can give it to our neighbors. It is good to help. Remember how the Lord took the fish and the bread and fed many people. You must have that same mindset. Helping people is all that really matters. The Lord said, "If you love Me, feed My sheep" (see John 21:17).

KEEP YOUR EYES OPEN

Dennis thought he was irreplaceable, so he never followed authority but did his own thing. He blamed his parents for his bad way of living. He never listened to his bosses and felt like the world was against him. If you refuse to listen to authority, you will refuse to listen to God. But it is time for you to open your eyes and see the world that God put around you. Stop following your pride and be a man. In other words, stop borrowing the eyes of others and grow up. When you do so, you can engage in a relationship with God. This is why you sometimes see people who are happy in a new relationship. They are finally seen and valued as God created them.

It's also why you see some other people loathe themselves because it's how they've been seen and treated in a relationship. But the Bible tells us a story about believers around the world that God has freed from enslavement in the past. He has been releasing people from the weight of painful situations and problems since the beginning of time. Perhaps you do not see it this way, but one thing is for sure: we know that God does not want your problem to hold you back. Take, for instance, holding on to your hurt, unforgiveness, or other dysfunctional ties to the past that certainly affect your present relationship. Sometimes, the way you deal with your issues and problems will affect your future as well. But the Lord will forgive you when you pray about your grief, pain, guilt, shame, or even your old style of living. Talk to God about your burden and your shame so your heart can be moved. But at the same time, I want you to follow His guidance so you can begin to experience more happiness, better relationships, and more fulfillment than you ever thought possible.

When You've Tried Everything
and Failed, Try the Lord

Jack and Wendy got married right after college. They both had good jobs. Their next goal was to have a baby, but that would take a miracle because they had been trying for the longest time with no results. Their church family prayed for them, and at the same time, they visited more than two specialists, but there was no good outcome. After a while, they both stopped trying. She started to feel sick, so she visited her doctor. Something amazing happened! She was pregnant. Everything was going well, but one day, she came home and saw a note on the bed: "I am sorry, Wendy. I am leaving you. I'll call you with my new phone number. We'll need to discuss the kids and finances. I am sorry that things are not working out for you and me."

It was two in the morning. Wendy was up. Sleep never visited her. She looked around the house. She saw pictures of herself, her husband Jack, and their kids on the walls. She felt sad and started to breathe heavily. Her eyes turned red, and she felt disoriented as if something foundational had suddenly crumbled from under her feet. She cried and looked around. Fear took over; she could feel the blood running through her veins. She was overwhelmed and hurt.

To get her mind off things, she looked around and started to take stock of things in the house. She believed in God. *This is just a test of faith. I know my Lord will take me through*, she thought. She loved Jack with all her heart, but people change. Jack was her soulmate and life partner. Looking back on the years they had been together, she cried. When they met, they both thought God had brought them together. She was sure of it. All the signs were there. She told herself this was a beautiful relationship. She said, "Something happened, but I cannot explain it because this man was a good father to our kids. How could this happen? It's like a nightmare."

Wendy was aware of some misunderstandings they had in the past. Sometimes, she felt miserable in the marriage, but she was trying to work on it. Some months ago, she had shut down and become distant and preoccupied, even cold. She cried herself to sleep at night. She could not reach him. They used to sit with each other in church and hold hands, but now they were sitting a million miles apart from each other. Jack made things more difficult. He started to spend more and more time at work.

They had been going through a lot of stress lately. Jack's company had presented him with an option to relocate to a different part of the country, which would give him a much better position with the company. It was a good opportunity for him not to get laid off. When the offer was on the table, the couple and their close friends discussed the proposition. After praying and fasting, a discussion was a good decision. When it came to the final moment, it was clear to them that moving was the best decision. Separation from their close friends and church family was very difficult for them. Now, they were in a different atmosphere. Jack had been trying to adjust to his work. It all came together. They spent weeks moving in, trying to enroll the kids in school, and at the same time, getting to know the area, meeting the neighbors, and finding a good church home in which they felt they belonged.

Everything was going so well; no one could tell when Jack started to distance himself or shut down from Wendy. She noticed it and thought she had a problem. She felt so bad and asked him if everything was okay. Most of the time, he said no. She suggested they see a counselor. Over time, they became strangers in the marriage.

They started to blame each other for moving. The relocation had taken its toll. However, they were having problems in their marriage long before it. She was in denial because the signs of discontent were all there, but she refused to pay attention to it. Wendy refused to surrender to God. She had certain spiritual blindness, and she had never allowed God to touch, help, or heal her. Wendy was one of those people who believed she could do it by herself, but when something bad happened, she refused to take responsibility for her life. In her mind, whenever a problem arose, it was always the fault of someone other than herself. The problem with Wendy was she liked to blame others and excuse herself. She refused to take the blame and admit that she was wrong. This condition was passed down from Adam and Eve and is in the world today. People point fingers at each other. The devil began the blame game. Genesis 3:12 (KJV) says, "And the man said, The woman whom thou gavest to be with me, she gave me of the tree, and I did eat."

Although Wendy had a severe case of spiritual blindness, she was in good company. Wendy encountered some challenges in life, but she was not a bad person. In fact, she was a good person at heart. She was a praying woman, and she loved God and her family and friends; she wanted the best for all of them. She was a hard-working wife, mother, and a good companion. Sometimes, when things went well, they went very well. At times, when problems arose, things got out of hand and went very badly. The first person to blame was Jack since he was the person closest to her.

Take, for instance, when she was overwhelmed with the kids, it was because Jack had his hands full, and he could not help. Wendy wanted it her way. She complained when they had financial struggles that Jack was not making enough. Sometimes, when Jack came from work, Wendy would want to talk to him, but Jack was so tired he would say she lacked concern for him. Sometimes, he disagreed with what she was saying, and she thought he wanted to control her. The worst part of the disagreement was when he mentioned something she did not like. Wendy would lose it and become enraged and accuse him of being critical and judgmental.

It came to a point where Jack had his share of responsibility as well. He tried his best to change to please her, but when he realized it was a waste of time and he could never please her, he pointed out some lack of responsibility in her, but she denied it and walked away. He tried to stand up as a man and be strong, not letting her know how much the way she treated him hurt. He thought he might have given up too soon. The relocation was not the only thing affecting their marriage; it was wounded a long time ago. She tried to blame the problems of relocation on Jack even though she was fasting and praying to hear from God for the answer.

Wendy told Jack that she did not like his job, and she started to blame him for not trying to find something better where they used to live. She was never pleased with Jack's decision. Jack started to blame himself. He wondered if he was not showing enough love to her or supporting her in her decision. When he looked back, whatever was wrong, it was always his fault. In fact, even before the breakup occurred, she was telling people about their marriage problems. Perhaps, they should have spoken with a family member or a friend, somebody who was around them for a long time, about their marriage dynamics. Wendy should have known that she was not perfect, but when something went wrong, she blamed Jack. She had difficulty owning her part in their struggle. Most likely, if someone approached her about all these problems, she would respond with, "But you don't understand what kind of man he is!" and then the conversation would go nowhere.

In fact, I thank God is working on their relationship. It is during hard times like this God does His best work. Remember when the children of Israel were coming from Egypt, they reached the Red Sea. They had nowhere to go, and God told Moses to stretch out his hand over the sea, and it was divided. If God can do that, He can also fix your relationship, so stay with the Lord, and He will make your dreams come true. Exodus 14:21 (KJV) says, "And Moses stretched out his hand over the sea; and the LORD caused the sea to go back by a strong east wind all that night, and made the sea dry land, and the waters were divided."

Sometimes, It Takes
a Sudden Upsetting

Most of the time, a sudden upsetting can help us face reality. Wendy was in denial for months and refused to consider that her constant blaming was at the heart of their marriage problems. It took her a while to see that her conduct hurt Jack so much that it made him doubt that he was loved by God or people around him, and it broke his heart. There were so many things going through Jack's mind. His plan was to file for bankruptcy. For the first time, Jack felt that he had a breakthrough, and the good thing about it was Wendy did not know about it. Jack called a friend; he helped him with the paperwork. Wendy was wondering what was going on. She waited until Jack left the house and went through Jack's papers.

Wendy told herself, "I am not filing for bankruptcy. I am going to have faith and wait on the Lord." Wendy did what people had been doing from ancient days. She did the one thing anyone should do when they are lost and cannot find themselves: she started to pray. Wendy started to reach out to God in a special way for help. There came a time when she heard nothing, felt nothing, but she never gave up. She realized that a time was coming that no one could stop her; that was a set time in her life. She kept on praying because she remembered God said He would never leave her or forsake her. She stood on that God's promise to take care of her. She knew that she did some things in the past that were not good, but God fixed her broken heart. Remember when Jesus said these words:

> Come to me, all who labor and are heavy laden, and I will give you rest. Take my yoke upon you, and learn from me, for I am gentle and lowly in heart, and you will find rest for your souls. For my yoke is easy, and my burden is light.
>
> Matthew 11:28-30 (ESV)

Wendy knew all these things would not happen overnight. She would have to wrestle for long periods of time as she reached out to God.

Wendy continued to pray, search, and listen for an answer. Within a few days, something began to happen in her heart. Psalm 73:26 (NIV) states, "My flesh and my heart may fail, but God is the strength of my heart and my portion forever." God started to talk to her heart, and she began to look back onto the whole saturation with Jack. She sat down and thought, *I am not hurting Jack; I am hurting myself.* She stopped feeling the pain Jack had caused her and, instead, felt the pain that she had caused Jack. She thought back on some conversation they had in the past. Jack had told her she was always blaming him for everything. She realized that was true. *In some of those situations, God was taking us through our wilderness,* she thought. She felt bad about the entire situation. She remembered the statements of blame in which she had made everything his fault. Wendy remembered that Jack had tried to point out her part in the problems, but she had simply ignored what he had to say.

One particular night in December, when it was so cool, Jack was going through some tough times, and he asked her to move closer to him in bed. That was one of the moments when he was feeling lots of job stress. Jack had asked her to cuddle with him in bed before they went to sleep. He was like a ten-year-old boy who needed some reassurance of love. He was asking for comfort to get through the night, but her response was not so polite. She had been so angry at him that she said, "If you handled your job better, you would be a man and not a workaholic." She was so upset she came off the bed and went to the neighboring room. She started to cry because of the things she said to Jack and apologized. She told Jack, "I feel the rejection and injury that I have caused you." She said, "When I take a clearer look at your perspective, I feel such remorse and anguish for your hurt. The truth is I put everything in this marriage, but I forgot the main ingredient is Jesus Christ."

Be Truthful to Yourself

There came a time when Wendy's heart was open for a couple of days. It was like a miracle. She was telling the truth about everything, including the way she treated her husband and her lack of responsibility in the relationship. She started to say bad things about herself and asked God for help and to show her the right way to live and serve Him. Wendy's thoughts and behavior reminded me of a statement in the Bible about the way we sometimes feel toward ourselves when we become aware of our sins. "When you become aware of your guilt in any of these ways, you must confess your sin" (Leviticus 5:5, NLT). Wendy kept on praying for God's help because she knew that a day was coming that no one could stop her.

Wendy started to come to herself. She began feeling some loving and positive movement. She started to look into the situation, and she discovered a deeper sense of appreciation and love for her husband. By telling the truth and looking to herself, she took responsibility for her part of the blame in the relationship. As a result, she could see more room inside her to see her husband's good parts and all those great things she married him for.

God started to talk into her spirit. The messages that God gave her started to make sense. Wendy now began to go by the word in the Bible: wife, obey your husband. Ephesians 5:22 (KJV) says, "Wives, submit yourselves unto your own husbands, as unto the Lord." All these things were going on in her head; they all seemed to be saying the same thing: go and apologize to your husband and make it right with him. Wendy did not know exactly how to start to apologize because of the situation.

She called Jack and asked to meet with him. It was so hard for her, but she did it. She tried to explain everything to him. She told him what happened to her as best she could and then sincerely apologized for the many years of heaping blame on him and for not acknowledging her own problem and trouble. She tried to conduct herself in the best possible way. Then, she departed. Wendy tried to make the conversation about her failures and nothing else as if she was talking to a friend. This was the most difficult conversation of her life.

Jack tried to be the more mature one. On his way to the meeting, Jack prepared himself for more cursing and blaming. As soon as Jack got there, he realized that Wendy was truly changed. He said to himself, "God must have done something to change her heart." When he saw her, he started to fall in love all over again. Jack tried to put everything aside and was willing to give her a second chance, and she wished to be back with him. They talked for a moment, and in a few weeks, he was back in the house where he belonged.

Their story had just begun. Wendy started to visit the church again. She realized how to take ownership of her own failings. The thing is to own your failure. It takes the Word of God to help someone change because people don't just own their failure like that. But with some counseling, Wendy realized, if she wanted her marriage to work, she would have to do more than take ownership for the pain she caused Jack. She needed to go into prayer and fasting and ask God to change her life, and at the same time, she needed to change her behavior.

There is nothing too hard for God to do. If He opened the eyes of the blind, God can do all things. All you have to do is surrender to Him, and He will change your life.

Wendy started to look back on her life and saw the things she was doing to herself and her husband. Wendy felt so bad about the entire situation and asked God to do a transformation in her life. It was a good thing Wendy was praying during this time because God had to keep softening her heart. Wendy said, "I really did not want to see the things about myself. I really needed to see in order to grow up and stop blaming the people around me." Wendy changed her perspective of the way she treated people and started to respect her marriage. Wendy cried when she looked back on the way she used to treat her kids. She said, "I should take ownership of how I parent my kids and the way it affected them." Her communication with people has improved. She is no longer alienating people with her behavior. She also apologized to all the people she blamed in the past and also asked them to stop her whenever she was out of line. She prayed and asked God for forgiveness for when she was cursing Him about the relocation and humbly told Him how grateful she was He had given her a second chance to do her marriage the right way.

This is a set time in their life. The couple went through so much, but there is a side benefit to all of this. Jack started to own up to his shortcomings in the relationship. Jack was no longer married to his job; he just worked the hours that he was supposed to work and went home to his family. Jack started to testify to his wife that when they had been having problems, he should have made better decisions. He felt like he had let her down. After putting an end to doubt and dispute, these two started down the right path toward becoming the couple they had always dreamed of becoming. These two people are working hard on their marriage. Both of them are reaching that maturity. But there is a time coming that no one can stop them, and that is a set time in their life. A time that God ordained for them, where no one can stop them. These two people reconciled their marriage and started to minister to other couples in significant ways. It is truly a set time for them.

It is truly a blessing for these two people. When Wendy prayed to God in the bathroom that day, she thought God would show Jack the things that were happening to them. God does not work on our time. Wendy might have been surprised by the way God answered her prayer. God showed her that she needed to learn to shoulder the burdens of ownership of her life. Just to show her the way that God planned for her, He had her go through a problem in her marriage, but there was a time that God set for the couple to come together again. He ordained it, but it is up to them to take the opportunity and walk in it. In Matthew 4:18, when Jesus called the disciples to be fishers of men, what if the disciples declined the call? Where would you and I be today? However, they took the opportunity and preached the gospel of Jesus Christ so that you and I have an understanding of it in our generation today.

The story of Wendy and Jack remained me of a story in the Bible. The story of Naaman, the captain, who was told to wash in the Jordan seven times. Naaman walked away because he did not want to go into Jordan River (2 Kings 5:10). When we pray, we do not get what we ask for. Wendy prayed to God for something, and God told her that she was the problem. That's the way God works, and that is a great illustration for you and me. If we do not get what we ask for, remember God knows best. I do believe that God has a set time for every human being on the earth to change their life in one way or another. Yet I can say I am part of that miraculous event because one day, God took me and transformed me, and today I can say, "What a mighty God we serve!"

I am so glad that God manifested Himself to Jack and Wendy and showed them that He was still with them all through their problem. Reflecting on everything that happened, I am glad it happened the way it did. For instance, Wendy's story helps us remember that we will never be able to predict what path or approach God will take. We will never be able to tell what God will do next in our life. He is a miracle-working God. There is a saying that the greatest miracles are often those God brings about in the quiet of the human heart. Jeremiah 29:11 (NIV) says, "'For I know the plans I have for you,' declares the LORD, 'plans to prosper you and not to harm you, plans to give you hope and a future.'"

The Principle of Responsibility

The story of Wendy and Jack is like reading a storybook. It basically tells us that when we live in this world, there will be problems. At the same time, you have to take responsibility for your actions. Wendy tried to live her life like a candle in the wind, and whenever she called on the Lord, He had to answer her immediately. Whatever decision God gives you or the situation you must resolve, it will play a part in you achieving your future goals. Proverbs 16:3 (ESV) says, "Commit your work to the LORD, and your plans will be established."

You can do all things through the strength of God, but at the same time, you have to put some willpower into it. It could not be further from the truth. It is the responsibility of God to take care of His children. There is a time that is set in our life when God determines how we must live and serve Him. He makes a way where there was no way; He puts food on our table and cloth on our backs. "Blessed be the name of the LORD from this time forth and for evermore. From the rising of the sun unto the going down of the same, the LORD's name is to be praised" (Psalm 113:2-3, KJV).

When a child of God engages in the work of the Lord, He will put the Holy Spirit at work in that person and let it be a success. He is a master builder, and we are His best job. God will do everything to protect us. He told us to put on the full armor and "pray in the spirit on all occasions with all kinds of prayers and requests. With this in mind, be alert and always keep praying for all the Lord's people" (Ephesians 6:18, NIV).

This will help a lot of wives and husbands to see that Wendy and Jack went through a bad situation but still kept their marriage. When you do your best, God will do the rest. God sent some people over their house, moved Jack out but not let him file for divorce, just to open the heart of Wendy. What did she do? She searched the Word of God and looked for words that lined up with her situation. She did not give up on God because she took responsibility and found the light that He was pointing her to.

In the end, the principle of responsibility is a matter of spiritual discernment. We all need to learn that God prepares a time, a set time for us to work in the other life.

TAKE RESPONSIBILITY
FOR YOUR FAULT AND BLAME

Some people struggle with telling the truth, and most of all, they always blame someone else for their problems. Sometimes, this hinders them from taking full responsibility for their situation. A man working for a company making boxes is late every morning because he sleeps late, and they fire him, and he says it is not his fault. Perhaps, it is a woman with a controlling husband who got a divorce; the husband says he is not the problem—she is.

Many people would disagree that we are the cause of all our problems. This is one of the responsibilities that we take: to live in a sinful world. In this sinful world, people refuse to take responsibility for their actions. Do not be innocent about it: people need to stop placing the blame on others and take responsibility for their actions. As ultimately, in terms of solving this issue, it is irrelevant who is innocent in life. If someone cares about the problem, he or she will set aside differences and work out the problem.

Some problems come to empower you, and some come to break you down. It is up to you to make the change. Many people own their problems, so they take a long time to go away. For instance, the Bible talks about a man named Nehemiah, who was enslaved, but he had a problem with the destruction of Jerusalem. He refused to live with it. He took the initiative and went to Jerusalem to rebuild it.

The problem will come, but there is a way you should handle it. There are some people who have problems but refuse to give up; take, for example, a jobless man who goes on many interviews but never gets a job. An unhappy wife seeking help goes to many friends, but she does not care whether or not her husband is interested. When problems come your way, you are free to take risks. Proverbs 3:5 says, "Trust in the LORD with all your heart, and do not lean on your own understanding." This is for people who like to take risks.

Feel Bad About the Gifts

It was in summer when my best friend Sam called to ask if we could meet for lunch. My wife said she sensed something was wrong. I saw him two months ago, but I was still looking forward to meeting with him. As I got there, we greeted each other at the door of the restaurant. Sam abruptly announced, "I lost my job." "Lost your job?" I was shocked. Sam was not some inexperienced young man fresh out of college and trying to establish himself in the workplace. He was a well-known manager who was very experienced, working in a manufacturing firm where he had been in that position for many years. He took pride in his job and planned to make it a lifetime career. Sam looked devastated. His mind was on his wife and their three children who depended on him. I said, "I am so sorry. What happened?"

He tried to explain what had happened. He told me when the old manager left, the company they hired a new boss at the upper levels. The new boss's name was Peter. They did not hit it off well. They had different management techniques. Sam was orderly and methodical, and Peter was more intense and challenging. Peter pushed Sam to take more risks, explore new ideas, and try different approaches with the people he managed. Sam looked into the whole situation and said, "This is not right." Peter was missing the importance of diligence, responsibility, he supposed to helping people do their jobs with excellence. Sam believed that Peter was rather unreasonable in his expectations. Sam did not like the way Peter did things, but he was trying to meet his boss's goals and expectations. Each time peter work on something it went wrong. Anyway, he has to go over it.

It will take me many painful attempts just to fix the problem. Sam told me that is boss calls him and let me go.

Sam calls me in the middle of the night, can you pray with me. So, we pray after praying I told him to read (Psalms 91:2). I will say of the Lord, He is my refuge and my fortress: my God in him will I trust.

The next day Sam calls me, I think God is trying to tell me something. Maybe He has a plan for me. I can tell you this is not a coincidence, but I have no clue as to what it all means." Sam told me, God said in His word He is my refuge.

I told him in a situation like this, God is the best person to rely on. He puts up kings and brings down kings. Blessed is the name of the Lord. "I told him I like your motivation Sam he said at this point, learning what God wants me to learn seems like the best thing for me.

I tried to call Sam twice a month just to see how he was picking up the pieces of his broken life. At the same time, I gained great admiration for my best friend Sam. When I looked back at the situation, I never saw Sam wallow in self-pity or blame the world for his downfall, but every day, he tried to get the full understanding of God's power and have the strength to keep him going through life. I prayed and asked God to help him find a job. His bills were coming in. He did not know what to do; he called his sister's husband is name is Sean. Sean said, "I was just about to call you. Someone just left my job, and I thought of you. Can you come over right away?" Sam says yes, he took the position and made the company a remarkable success, and he is still there today, doing well. Romans 8:31 (KJV) says, "What shall we then say to these things? If God be for us, who can be against us?"

How God Works

As Sam thought back, he tried to do everything by the books because he knew he had a family to take care of and bills to pay. If you ask me, I think the best thing Sam should do is give God the praise. Just to show you how God works, things will go wrong in your life, but there is a time coming when no one can stop you; that is a set time that God ordained. You can see that Sam got the full knowledge of how God works. He took himself out of the situation and depended on God to work. Sam recognized that his knowledge and high intelligence could not help him get a job. He opened his heart and welcomed God in to do the work, which took him to a place where he could put his trust in the God who parted the Red Sea. Sam came to the understanding that man can give people jobs, but the pay will not be good enough, but when God gives you a job, you will not have room to contain your pay. Sam read the Bible and asked people to pray for him.

You and I can do the same thing. God answered Sam's prayer. When the situation first began, Sam did not know it would change, but God did! Sam learned that Peter was not his enemy. Peter was the one who took Sam to the presence of God. In looking at the situation from a different perspective, Peter thought he was doing wrong to Sam, but he basically was the one who helped Sam to know God. Sam was not taking any chances. He remembered what happened, so he stayed in line and kept the faith. He knew there was not a lot of room for mistakes, so he kept on praying for the power of God to work on his behalf.

Sam understood his problems and remembered that Jeremiah 1:5 (KJV) says, "Before I formed thee in the belly I knew thee; and before thou camest forth out of the womb I sanctified thee, and I ordained thee a prophet unto the nations." He went to work with a smiling face because he knew that God was with him. It took a lot of patience and effort, but in the end, Sam was a new man.

You can count on Sam. He is still the same person, reliable and responsible. Sam is taking it one day at a time. Whenever Sam visits the church, he seems alive on the inside. There are so many improvements he made in his life. Now, he is trying new things. Sam is now open for advice. When he looked back at where God brought him from, he discovered that he has a talent for helping people with business. Sam volunteers at the church that he attends. He volunteers there to mentor men who need career assistance, and he loves doing it. Sam went down, but he did not stay down. With God's help, he elevated himself to the top.

Understanding Your Problem

When we look back on everything, we notice we all have problems like Sam. Unfortunately, it is a part of life. But the way we approach our problems places us into two groups: those who have the problems and those who let the problems have them. Group one looks death in his eyes and keeps on going, and the next group gives up as they hear about the problem. But there are some people like Sam who find something useful in the problem and use it to go forward in life, but in order for that to happen, they must put their trust in the true and living God. Sometimes, the problem relates to your job, relationship, or your health. Sometimes, as family members, we all tend to fight to put out the fire and make sure it does not flare up again. Sometimes, it may be a sickness from the past that came back with a stronger force and causes pain all over your body, and at the same time, your marriage is falling apart. With all these problems, it is very painful, and you want the pain to go away; that is your biggest concern. (Philippians 4:13 KJV) say I can do all things through Christ which strengtheneth me.

There is nothing wrong with trying to get rid of your problems and resisting the pain. In order for us to come out of our problems, we must make the first step, and God will see our difficulties very differently than we see them. Sometimes, the problems we go through are a gift from God because they bring us to Him. In the Bible, Job lost everything, but that did not stop him from serving the Lord. Problems will come, but when we are under the umbrella of God, when the rain falls, whether it is hot or cold water, God will take care of us. He loves us so much He wants to elevate us and let us shine like a light in a dark place. He has many plans and lessons for us, but first, we must go through some problems.

The word "illuminate" is important here, for God is not as concerned with getting us out of problems as He is in letting us shine through our problems. Because of that, God allows you and me to be illuminated, and when we do so, all our problems can disintegrate. And when all of that disintegrates, we must have a positive mindset and remember the One who delivered us out of our problems. Share your testimony and let others know who helped you.

Have compassion for others just like Jesus. Scripture states that Jesus demonstrated the power of God. He had compassion for the hungry and fed them all: He healed the blind, raised the dead, cast out demons, and cleansed the lepers. Jesus was always touched by the spirit of compassion when He saw His people like sheep without a shepherd. This is why we read in the Bible, "My brethren, count it all joy when ye fall into divers temptations; Knowing this, that the trying of your faith worketh patience" (James 1:2-3, KJV).

You Cannot Solve It by Yourself

Trouble is, by definition, something that you cannot solve. If you could have fixed it, you probably would have. You may be struggling, and all of your attempts to resolve it are not enough. Trouble brings us to the end of ourselves. It can exhaust our resources, our strength, our will, and also our mood. Sometimes, it is not good to be at the end of ourselves because we can feel helpless, lost, fearful, and disoriented, not knowing where to turn. If we keep on feeling sorry for ourselves or bemoaning how helpless we are, we are truly in a bad spot. However, we can take a different direction.

The Lord knows that we cannot control troubles, so Jesus tells us in John 14:1 (KJV), "Let not your heart be troubled. Believe in God; believe also in me. In my father's house are many rooms. If it were not so, would I have told you that I go to prepare a place for you?" Sometimes, we can allow our troubles to turn us upward so that we can shift our focus off the things that God have for us. Trouble gives us an opportunity to look beyond our small minds, our friends, answers, and trusted habits and peer out into the unknown, where God will take you to the place, He planned for you. When we are at the end of the rope and there's nowhere to turn, God steps in and changes things around because He is God. God knows everything. When trouble comes our way, we look up and down for help. We search all over just to hear a voice say, "Come," but all we have to do is look forward to the One who knows our troubles, the solutions, the lessons, and the ways. The on-time God is always there for us.

We are in a time in our life where we have to play it safe. In a time like this, we do not need a god that is made out of wood because when we get hungry, we will make fire with it. We need a God who is there for us. I am talking about the God of Daniel, Isaac, and Moses. We would rather keep things under our control and worship the true and living God, but at the same time, God knows the approach to take what is drying up our soul; He will work it out in His best interest to help us. God wants us to look upward to all His blessings, opportunities, and love. God will work like a cloudburst raining down on thirsty land that did not receive rain in a thousand years. But as the great movement starts, it forces into the debris and breaks up the clog; now freshwater starts to renew the stream in your life. When we pay attention to God's Word and look upward, we open up to God, and He also opens Himself up to us.

The next step is to pay attention to the soul of man because the soul of man never dies. The transformation we go through in our spiritual life does not end there. Our soul has to get ready to engage in the transformation to eternal life. Once the trouble starts, God takes us through a journey into ourselves to demonstrate what He wants us to learn. God is constantly teaching us, helping, guiding, and encouraging His people to let them have an understanding of what is going on around them and to change their attitudes. He wants them to react to the positive action around them so the inner man can work on the heart. It is like a shining bright light in a dark place. In order for that to happen, we must first submit our heart to Him, and He will take the weaknesses out.

When the weak heart gets ironed out by God, most of those people try to get married; as a result, their marriage may end in divorce, even if they have been married before. In order for some of them to get married again, they need to clean their heart because they have experienced some relationship that was not of God. Some of those relationships were like an emotional train wreck. Remember, the heart is where love comes from, and if it does not work for you, please do not form various attitudes. Most people address the problem by shutting down themselves and giving up on love. Most of them live feeling sorry for themselves.

Some people never take the time to pray and ask the Lord to send them a loving person. But some take the attitude saying, "I do not care how the person looks; it is better than being alone." Some people never take the time to consult their heart; they just want a spouse by dating someone they're drawn to for some unknown reason and marrying that person.

None of these people are consulting their heart, and here comes the trouble. Some of these people take the heart check, praying and asking God to send them the right person in their life. Some of them can remember what happened in the train-wreck marriages in the past: breakups and disappointments. Some of them pray night and day, asking God for help because they do not want to contribute to the problem of bad relationships and not let them be drawn to the wrong person. They are also asking God to help them make the change in order for them to pick the right person. These people know that they cannot do it on their own, so they give it to God because God knows our heart, and it bears a lot of good fruit. The Bible tells us we must be careful who we marry, so we must be careful in whom we pick to love.

Because human being says one thing and do different thing. It's possible that when we think about the soul, we can take our attention to when the Lord said He does not judge on the outward part of man but the inside. Psalm 16:10 (KJV) says, "For thou wilt not leave my soul in hell; neither wilt thou suffer thine Holy One to see corruption."

One writer told us you don't have a soul. You are a soul. You have a body. So the reaction that occurs in our bodies is not always under our control. Because many areas of our lives are subject to God, He builds it up, and He breaks it down. It is important for people to discover that they are not just anybody, but they are part, made in the image of the Holy Trinity because, in Genesis 1:26 (KJV), God said, "Let us make man in our image."

So, we are wonderfully made in the image of God, the bible told us that we are powerful people in God. God love us so much that He set us apart for himself (Psalm 4:3 KJV) but know that the Lord hath set apart him that is Godly for himself; the Lord will hear when I call unto him. He will never withhold any good things from you He told us that we are the apple of His eyes. (Psalm 107: 31 KJV) say oh that men would praise the Lord for His goodness, and for His wonderful works to the children of men..

Your Day Is Coming

No one calls for trouble to come their way, but it comes. It can be there for more than one reason. Some people use trouble as a gift to structure their life and help them normalize the situation taking over their life. Physical suffering is a regular part of every human being's life. Jesus told us that we will face many things on this earth (Peter 3:21 KJV) say for even hereunto were ye called: because Christ also suffered for us, leaving us an example, that ye should follow His step. God know what we are going through so, when physical suffering and struggle start, we most not complain about the situation that these things should not be. However, the Lord told us that we will go through trouble and trial, but He will be there for us. Life is difficult. We must try to resist the bad thing that comes our way; we must pray to the Highest God to help us face the reality of physical suffering.

Sometime when we suffering God is trying to tell us something it looks bad, we do not see no way out but that the time God work is best miracle. When Christian suffers for Christ, He gave back double for your trouble. When Job lost everything, God gave back double of everything's. Remember His Word! You will go through difficulties, but God will be there with you. God never said it would be easy. Since physical suffering is a part of us, God sees ultimate reality as it is, and at the same time, when God speaks to us, we must respond in a positive manner, not trying to have an argument with Him because we are sick and going through pain.

In our conversation with others, we must remember the physical suffering in the world today. We must make a choice to lend a hand in physical suffering because those are the opportunities that

God gives us. This is our time now to step out and lend a hand to people who are suffering. The Lord says, "If you love Me, feed My sheep." To prove your love to the Lord, take the opportunities and step out and lend a hand. Because we do not know what tomorrow will bring, we are up and going and, in a few seconds, we are dawn. There are many missionaries go around the world who suffer and died and never get the chance to return home (2 Corinthians 4: 17 KJV) say for our light affliction, which is but for a moment worketh for us a far more exceeding and enteral weight of glory. . After all the suffering on this earth God will call us to be with angle in heaven no sickness are pain.

LIVING IN SUFFERING

Troubles coming your way to help you grow stronger. Sometimes, they help you get a picture of what Jesus went through. Christs go through the cross so you and I can live in this world. (Luke 14: 27 KJV) say and whosoever doth not bear His cross and come after me cannot be my disciple. The bible told us that things is going to come our way that we cannot understand so God send is son to help us. All the problem and suffering start in the Garden of Eden and spill into our generation. So, our life changes human being of to live in this sinful world until Christ return. Christs have a set time for His coming when the gospel preached in all the world. (Revelation 22:20 KJV) say he who testifies to these things says, surely, I am coming quickly Amen even so come Lord Jesus.

Some people say life is not fear, but we all are going through the same things in different way. (St John 16: 33 KJV) say these things I have spoken unto you that in me ye might have peace in the world ye shall have tribulation but be of good cheer I have overcome the world. If Jesus did not overcome this world, where will you and I be today. The darkness would cover us up and take us into the pit of hell. The light of the glorious gospel shine in our heart and prepare us for heaven.

Jerusalem was a beautiful place to live. When Jesus saw their hard-heartedness, He ached to gather its people as a hen covers its chicks under her wings, but they refused His love (Mathew 23:37). God's response to the trouble He was facing was that He took responsibility for doing something about it. God is a man of integrity. He does not avoid, deny, or misunderstand the meaning of trouble. Due to that fact, Christ suffered during the process. Unfortunately, at the same time that Christ was redeeming, restoring, forgiving, repairing, and healing us, the enemy still came against Him. As physical beings, we can learn something from the Lord. He addresses the trouble His way so that we can identify or associate ourselves with His suffering. The study of God's Word never stops. He gives man the knowledge to engage spiritually, to identify with His pain, to be closer to Him, to see reality as it is, and to take the right approach to life.

The troubles and trials we face today are lessons for our tomorrow. They will allow us to come closer to God's suffering, especially through Jesus, "the author and perfecter of our faith, who for the joy set before Him endured the cross" (Hebrews 12:2, BSB). So when we identify ourselves with God's sufferings, we are deepened and matured. First Peter 4:13-16 (NIV) says,

> But rejoice inasmuch as you participate in the sufferings of Christ, so that you may be overjoyed when his glory is revealed. If you are insulted because of the name of Christ, you are blessed, for the spirit of glory and of God rests on you. If you suffer, it should not be as a murderer or thief or any other kind of criminal, or even as a meddler. However, if you suffer as a Christian, do not be ashamed, but praise God that you bear that name.

Many people who have been down this path will let you know that the trouble you face helps you start an ultimate learning process about God's suffering.

It is good to be a part of His life. Trouble helps us grow in Christ. Do not ask Him to remove it. He knows that if He takes it away, many people will stop praying. Some people's lives move forward with trouble. It helps them go forward in Christ. When trouble comes to some people, they pray and fast night and day until they hear from God.

How to Bear up under Suffering

Some people have the tendency to approach trouble like they know what they are doing. Trouble is the respect of no one when it come your way only one person can help you and His name is Jesus. It is a learning process some people learned lessons, such as how to have patience, and that is just part of the situation. Some of us refuse to go through the lesson and do bad things to their life. When you pray and ask God to bear you up in the time of trouble and suffering, He will. (Psalms 30: 8 KJV) say I cried to thee, o Lord; and unto the Lord I made supplication.

God helps us grow strong in bad times. Physical suffering will come, but we can ask God to help us in those bad situations because the longer we stay with God, the more we experience His love. Trouble will always show up, but the great professional at work, His name is Jesus. The bible told us about Hagar her life was hard she was a slaved. God spoke to in a remarkably way in her suffering. She was cast out and put in the wilderness because of the thing she did with Abraham. The Lord care for her, she says even in my trial and suffering the Lord is with me. The Lord never give up on no one He will do any thing to win you back to him. (Luke 15:10 KJV) say likewise I say unto you, there is joy in the presence of the angels of God over one sinner that repentant. Hagar was put out be man but was take up by God because the Lord see her heart. She was abandoned spiritually and emotionally and suffer in an indescribable way. Because someone use her against her will and she was punishing

for what someone did to her.

Enjoy Life As It Comes

I can remember the day when my sister announced that her husband James has a disease called osteopenia. Osteopenia is a bone disease. It means that your bones are too porous. Osteopenia, a precursor to the better-known osteoporosis, can lead to easy fracturing and slow healing of the bone. He told my sister that a couple of years ago, he was in a car accident, and he broke some bones in his body. Having learned what was going on, his doctor told him that his broken bones were a result of his condition.

He did not stop there. He took the situation in hands, started to investigate the cure for his diagnosis, and looked for treatments. He did something very clever and asked his entire family member about this disease. He discovered that his mother has osteoporosis, and the disease has not been easy for her to live with. James cried night and day to ask God to help him because he did not want to grow old with brittle bones.

James said, "This is not a surprise to me. The medical world has advanced to do many things to help this condition." Many doctors recommend certain supplements that can help, but exercises are very important to help strengthen the bones. His doctor is a man of God. He spent much time with him. The doctor put him on a regimen built around those factors.

James gives God praises every day that he followed this course of action so that things can improve for him. He said, "If it wasn't for God's will, the things I'm doing would not have actually worked. Along with everything that I am doing, it is important to measure the treatment's effectiveness. One day while James was reading the bible he come to (Jeremiah 32:17 KJV) say ah Lord God behold, thou hast made the heaven and the earth by thy great power and stretched out arm, and there is nothing too hard for thee.

James say it is very hard to live this way, not knowing what the next move should be, but with the love of the Lord I know one day all of this will over. He tried to keep up with the supplements and exercises, but in reality, he said, "I do not know how I am doing. This sickness keeps me going. I asked the doctor if it was possible to have more immediate feedback." James told me that he wanted to monitor himself more closely. The way medical science is going, I think they have the ability to do the best job. I told him to stick to the regimen and hope things would get better one day.

James told my sister that he has faith. James looked on the situation. He said, "I think I just find myself caught up in something that will offer me some benefits." James prayed and asked God to show him the right way to deal with this problem. James 5:14 (KJV) says, "Is any sick among you? Let him call for the elders of the church; and let them pray over him, anointing him with oil in the name of Lord." I try to support him by letting him know that there is a time coming that no one can stop him, and that is a set time that God ordained.

He said that I deeply believe in God's ability to work miracles and in His instantaneous, supernatural activities with us. I also believe that the normal way that God deals with us involves a sequence of events, a process that God directs and that we are to obey. Sometimes, we have to discipline ourselves in order to get involved in God's business. Exodus 23:25 (KJV) says, "And he shall bless thy bread, and thy water; and I will take sickness away from the midst of thee."

Although the Lord is my strength, I have to wait on him patiently because time is the field in which God has chosen to operate to get things done. Look into this: God made the universe in stages. It took the Israelites forty years to enter the promised land. It took many years before the true Messiah was born. Take a look at the Bible. There are many more examples of how God factors time into the way He works to care for us. We try to do things on our time. God does not go by our time because we want things to go our way right now and cannot wait. We also love instant answers, changes, and deliverance for ourselves. The Bible told us in Isaiah 40:31, "But they who wait for the LORD shall renew their strength; [...] they shall run and not be weary; they shall walk and not faint." God works on His own time. There are times we pray, and it seems like God does not hear us. This is what I see over and over again. God gave us the things we did not ask for, and many people get upset, but in the long run, it saves our lives. What a mighty God we serve! Sometimes, the situation is so bad that God takes more time to work on some of us.

God chooses us from the beginning of time, and we must serve Him with a true heart. It will take time. To live with Him for those long periods of time requires patience. For example, to make us accessible to God in all the ways needed to bring about His glory, we need to make ourselves more exposed to His love, grace, and truth, and He will start working inside of us. We must engage more in His Word, and we will learn things that will blow our minds. He will also give you a new heart and renew a right spirit in you. Get yourself ready and able to make use of the help God is offering you. As we are humans, our physical body teaches us that healing and change take time. Take, for instance, when Naaman was told to go in Jordan and dip himself seven times. He was complaining. He said, "With all the rivers, why Jordan?" God knows best. Second Kings 5:14 (KJV) says, "Then went he down, and dipped himself seven times in Jordan, according to the saying of the man of God: and his flesh came again like unto the flesh of a little child, and he was clean."

WAIT ON GOD

It is nice to be included. Time waits on no man. Sometimes, we are like children: that part of us that demands to have things fixed right away. In reality, sometimes, we feel stress, discouraged, frustrated, and ready to cry. Sometimes, we may find our way in which we try to work around the reality of time's. For instance, some people will feel a desperate need for immediate relief from a painful situation. Meanwhile, others have a strong belief that God will take care of them and bring instant deliverance if they wait on him. Isaiah 40:31 (KJV) says, "But they who wait for the LORD shall renew their strength; they shall mount up with wings like eagles; they shall run and not be weary; they shall walk and not faint." As a child of God, sometimes, you feel out of control when you cannot get things to speed up.

Some of us can understand that we are just human but are impatient, so they cannot wait as the Bible told us to wait. However, some people who can submit to the restriction of the Word generally find better results than those who protest or try to get around the situation. The fact still remains when humans insist on taking shortcuts and try to get quick fixes, they tend to repeat the same problem more than once. God told us in His Word that in order for you to resist the temptation of quick fixes, you have to develop a mind of patience. If God gave you a test, it will require time, and God is very patient. In other words, those things that are emergencies to us God has already fixed because they are not that important to Him. When God gave you a time factor, those things are intended to be more meaningful and significant to Him. For instance, there are some people whose financial dreams are built on winning the Powerball.

On the other hand, there are those who spend years training, getting experience, learning, and excited how to put a well-designed business together. The Bible tells us about these people in Proverbs 21:5 (ESV), which states, "The plans of the diligent lead surely to abundance, but everyone who is hasty comes only to poverty." Sometimes, when looking back at how people do things, I say to myself, "Why can't they wait and do it the right way?" Humanity never does things the right way, so God sent His Son to the earth just to get the job done the right way. At times, when it seems like nothing is going on in our life, the gift of faith is working to bring us closer to God.

This is what the kingdom of God is like. A man scatters some seeds on the ground; the seeds are growing right in front of his eyes, but he cannot tell if they are growing or not (see Mark 4). It is the same way with prayer. Someone prays for you; you cannot see the prayer at work, but the healing is taking place. What a mighty God we serve! Thank you, Father. You have given us the keys to the kingdom of heaven, and whatever we bind on the earth shall be bound in heaven, and whatever we loose on the earth shall be loosed in heaven (Matthew 16:19).

Sometimes, we take things for granted. Have you ever wondered why God gives so much to us? Everyone has their own opinion. The truth is God could have left the world flat and gray, but He chose not to leave us. We wouldn't have known the difference, but God loves us so much.

The Bible describes us in different ways. Let me start by telling you who you are. You are an heir of God and a coheir with Christ (Romans 8:17). You are eternal, like an angel (Luke 20:36). You have a crown that will last forever (1 Corinthians 9:25). You are a holy priest (1 Peter 2:5), a treasured possession (Exodus 19:5). But more than any of the above—more significant than any title or position—is a simple fact that you are God's child. As a result, if something is important to you, it's important to God. God makes us serve Him and live on this earth. A friend of mine thinks differently. After he visited a church, he told me some stories that are not in the Bible. So I correct him our relationship was not doing good so I, though he research and find the answer. He became distant for a while. I remember trying to fix things as quickly as I could so our friendship could get back to normal, but it just did not happen that way. He called me one day. He said, "I needed time to allow myself to see the light. I would rather not visit you until I feel better. Pray for me that God makes a way for me. I am working on changing my ways and the things that I have done to hurt you so it wouldn't happen again." We stayed in touch and kept talking to each other two times a month about the Bible. The situation was getting a little better until he started to go back to the conversation in the past.

One day, while we were on the playground, I made an offhanded remark, and the moment I heard it leave my lips, I remembered the consequence. I was so sick inside that I wondered if I had repeated the same thing all over again.

My friend took a look at me and saw the anxiety and apparently knew what was going on in my mind. He came off the playground and said, "Look, I didn't even think about what you said until I noticed your face." He said, "I had put all of that behind me; it's time to go forward."

Colossians 3:13 (KJV) says, "Forbearing one another [...] if any man have a quarrel against any: even as Christ forgave you, so also do ye."

The thing that helped us tolerate each other was telling ourselves that God loves us both the same way. The situation helped both of us to become actively engaged in the Word of God. The Word helped us experience how a friend in the name of God should conduct themself. Whenever we study the Word of God, we must use it to help save a soul. For instance, when we work with God, our work becomes easier: He will participate and give us a helping hand. Sometimes, we can feel helpless and out of control, but we can turn to the One who is fully in control and perfectly able to help in our times of need. Remember that "God is our refuge and strength, a very present help in trouble" (Psalm 46:1, KJV). To all my readers, whatever you are going through, God will send help one day because He is a kind and loving God.

You Are God's Idea

It is easy to wait on God, but what are you doing for yourself? When Moses went back to Egypt and engaged with the pharaoh, he called to God, and the Lord said to him, "What do you have in your hand?" In order for you to get things done, sometimes you have to bring something to the table. When Jesus visited the wedding, and they announced there was no more wine, Jesus told them to fill waterpots with water. And they filled them up to the brim (John 2:7). Some people think all they need to do is be patient and wait, and God will take care of everything their heart desires. The Bible never told us that. Some people believe that they must open their hands, and food will come to them. Some people wait for God to change things around, but at the same time, they are waiting for someone to open the door for them.

In the time we live, people are afraid to take the initiative and open the door of life for themselves. They wait on some prophecy to tell them to open the door of their life. I am not saying that God does not help us, but people must step out as children of God and open the door for themselves. Everyone wants the blessing of the Lord, but no one wants to go through the bad times. Remember Job, when he went through some bad times, God was with him. I was talking to a church friend of mine one day. He told me the way God helped Job was the same way He helped him. I told him, "Remember God said Job was a righteous man," and he stopped talking. It is easy to talk about Job's situation because it ended well. No one wants to be Samson because of his situation. Everyone wants to be Job, but remember both of them were in a bad situation. One remained faithful to God, and the other one kept on doing things out of the will of God. Stay faithful to the Lord, and He will give you your heart desire so you can give a testimony about His goodness. Psalm 145:8 (KJV) says, "The LORD is gracious and full of compassion; slow to anger and of great mercy."

Each Number Has Its Role

I would like to place emphasis on the spiritual significance of numbers and their perfect relationship to the Bible. This consistency that is found in the Scriptures and all the teachings will provide an inspiration helping us follow God and His work of directing our lives. From the beginning of time, numbers have played a very important role in God's business. The Bible tells us when Moses wrote the first five books of the Bible, they contained numbers.

Take, for instance, this fivefold division. It has a meaning intimately connected with the subjects of the books themselves. Genesis, which stands first among the books, has for its special line of truth what would be suggested by the name number one. Genesis tells us that God created the world. Genesis 1:2 (KJV) says, "And the earth was without form, and void; and darkness was upon the face of the deep. And the spirit of God moved upon the face of the waters."

Exodus is the second book that Moses wrote; it gave us knowledge of God's people leaving Egypt to go to the promised land. It also tells us that there were fights and struggles, but God was with them. Exodus 3:10 (KJV) says, "Come now therefore, and I will send thee unto Pharaoh, that thou mayest bring forth my people the children of Israel out of Egypt."

Leviticus, the third book, gives you a deeper insight into the further events; it also gives you knowledge of the divine-human relationship codified on Mount Sinai. Leviticus also tells us that the Lord spoke to Moses many different times to speak to Israel. Leviticus 4:2 (KJV) says, "Speak unto the children of Israel, saying, If a soul shall sin through ignorance against any of the commandments of the LORD concerning things which ought not to be done, and shall do against any of them."The book of Numbers is the fourth book; it contains the fulfillment of the promises to Abraham that his descendants would be the people of God and occupy the land of Canaan. Israel was so disobedient to God they murmured and complained against Moses and Aaron, so God let them wander in the wilderness. Numbers 14:33 (KJV) says, "And your children shall wander in the wilderness forty years and bear your whoredoms until your carcasses be wasted in the wilderness."

Deuteronomy is book number five: this book contains laws. Deuteronomy 17:19 (KJV) says, "And it shall be with him, and he shall read therein all the days of his life: that he may learn to fear the LORD his God, to keep all the words of this law and these statutes, to do them."

People from different cultures say there is no language without some numerals. In every human being's life and language, numbers have a definite place. In the earliest form of life, humans developed a method of counting by using their fingers. It has been stated that the system of mathematics was developed by the ancient Egyptians and also the Babylonians.

In ancient times, the Hebrews and Semites only used the decimal system, which involved using ten fingers. In the Hebrew language, they have no separate symbols for numbers. They use the same letters from the alphabet for their learning. The same Hebrew letter also stands for a certain number, and that was called the numerical value of a certain letter.

When the Sumerians introduced the mathematics system to the Babylonians through its development, these principles have influenced the measurement of time and space in the western world.

God inspired man to write the Bible. He also gives man the knowledge and understanding to use numbers in a way that could help them strengthen their lifestyle. For example, number three represents the Father, the Son, and Holy Spirit, three in one. It is the number in the Bible that stands for unity. Unity is an important biblical doctrine. It also symbolizes the unity of God. According to the Trinity doctrine, the Father is God, the Son is God, and the Holy Spirit is God. 1 John 5:7 (KJV) says, "For there are three that bear record in heaven, the father, the Word, and the Holy Ghost: and these three are one." In Ephesians 4:3, Paul admonished them to keep the unity of the Spirit in the bond of peace.

The Bible told us in John 17:21-22 (KJV) that when Jesus prayed, he said that they all are one "As thou, Father, art in me, and I in three, that they also may be one in us […] and the glory which thou gavest me I have given them; that they may be one, even as we are one." Some people do not understand how one man became three. The works of God are a mystery. Jesus prayed to His Father. He wants all His people to have unity. He also prayed that His people be one. Ephesians 4:6 (KJV) says, "One God and Father of all, who is above all, and through all, and in you all."

When Jesus was about to go on the cross, He took three of His followers with Him. Matthew 26:37 (KJV) says, "And he took with him Peter and the two sons of Zebedee, and began to be sorrowful and very heavy." When the Bible talks about number three, we must remember the three peoples that populate the earth after the flood. I am talking about Noah's three sons: Ham, Shem, and Japheth.

The Number Two Stands for Union, Division, Witnessing

The number two first speaks of unity and order. It also speaks of division and desolation. In the book of Genesis, God created two human beings. Genesis 1:27 (KJV) says, "So God created man in his own image, in the image of God created he him: male and female created he them."

The Bible tells us that there is a symbolic significance in the fact that Jesus sent His disciples forth two by two. Two also stands for witnesses that confirmed the truth, and their testimony, which otherwise would have been weak, was made strong. The number two meant augmented strength, redoubled energy, confirmed power.

Genesis 2:24 (KJV) says, "Therefore shall a man leave his father and his mother, and shall cleave unto his wife, and they shall be one flesh." The Bible tells us that the number two stands for the unity of marriage, "and they shall be one flesh." Here we have a man and a woman: two joined together by God to become one.

Ephesians 5:32 (KJV) says, "This is a great mystery: but I speak concerning Christ and the church." The Bible tells us that the union of Christ and the church shows us the power and strength we possess when we are joined unto Christ.

The Bible tells us about the union of two natures in man. When the old nature is broken down by the new nature, we possess power and strength in the Lord.

Some people do not believe in the union of death and life in the atonement of Christ, as seen in the two birds in Leviticus 14:4

(KJV): "Then shall the priest command to take for him that is to be cleansed two birds alive and clean, and cedar wood, and scarlet, and hyssop." It also goes on to tell us about the two goats in Leviticus 16:5 (KJV): "And he shall take of the congregation of the children of Israel two kids of the goats for a sin offering, and one ram for a burnt offering."

Revelation 11:3 (KJV) says, "And I will give power unto my two witnesses, and they shall prophesy a thousand two hundred and threescore days, clothed in sackcloth."

The Bible tells us about two arks: the ark of Noah's a beautiful type of Christ. Genesis 6:14 (KJV) says, "Make thee an ark of gopher wood: rooms shalt thou make in the ark, and shalt pitch it within and without with pitch." It provided absolute safety for all who abode within, but it could help no one outside. The next one is the ark of Bulrushes. Exodus 2:3 (KJV) says,

> And when she could not longer hide him, she took for him an ark of bulrushes, and daubed it with slime and with pitch, and put the child therein; and she laid it in the flags by the river's brink.

It was neither big nor strong, but it was safely sealed; as long as baby Moses stayed in, the mighty water stayed out.

Genesis 19:15 (KJV) says, "And when the morning arose, then angels hastened Lot, saying Arise, take thy wife and thy two daughters, which are here; lest thou be consumed in the iniquity of the city." The Bible tells us about the separation of Lot and his daughters from those who were destroyed in their sins. In the book of Genesis, chapter nineteen, you can see many works of the number two. It will give you knowledge of how God works and will put things in the right perspective.

Genesis 19:1 (KJV) says, "And there came two angels to Sodom at even: and Lot sat in the gate of Sodom; and Lot seeing them rose up to meet them; and he bowed himself with his face toward the ground." Also, Genesis 19:4 (KJV) says, "But before they lay down, the men of the city, even the men of Sodom, compassed the house round, both old and young, all the people from every quarter." Time and numbers are the context God uses to set a time in your life. Take hold of the great lesson that they teach us. We must let it help us learn God's ways and use them to make something in our lives. We must use them in a way that is better than it was before the time of change and growth even began.

To go forward, we can always be sure of this: As we walk through life doing our part and allowing the numbers of life to work some great changes in us, the God who inhabits eternity at our side does His deep transforming work. Of this, we can be sure. He will never leave us or forsake us.

Work with God

When I first got baptized, I was on the usher team in the church I attended. When people came to visit the church, we helped them to their seats, and if they needed prayer or spiritual help, we brought them to the pastor. The team worked with those people in whatever ways we could.

It was a pleasure for us to be helping people who make themselves available so God can use them to take the next step of faith. It felt so good to be present at some time in a person's life. It was the third Sunday of the second month of the year when Jackie came to the front in tears about an issue involving her teenage daughter, Pam. Her daughter was rebellious, doing drugs, and had major problems in school. She resisted any advice or help from Jackie. She disregarded her intentionally or made excuses so that she would not have to talk to her. Jackie thought just like any other parent would. She wanted her daughter to serve God and have her life straightened out, so the altar team prayed with her and tried to assist her in any way they could.

Two weeks later, Jackie came up to me with the same problem. A few weeks later, in the Bible class, she came to me again. Then, she asked me if we could talk about her problems when there was more time. We agreed to meet for brunch. By talking to Jackie, I learned she is a single mom who works at night to make ends meet while trying to raise her daughter. Jackie told me it was hard for her to ask for prayer in church because of her daughter's problem. At the same time, she was wondering if she was making a bigger deal out of this. We all talked to her, letting her know that having a child who is struggling is no laughing matter.

Jackie believed that when she walked up to the front of the church, God would make some changes in her life and also her daughter's life. I told her, "I am happy for you to make the first move because God will never impose on anyone. God gives a human being a mind of their own, knowing that if you are serious about Him, God is always ready to accept you. Faith and love will help you take the next step in the family of Christ."

The usher team hugged her, prayed for her, and said, "We believe in you. We all know that you love God. God loves you, too, because when you were going through your problem, He was there with you."

The conversation kept going.

"I would like you to think about something. Do you love God enough for Him to help you?"

Jackie looked at me like she saw a ghost. "I am not getting it," she said. "The day I went up to the front of the church, I gave Him my whole life. I never hold back on God, and there is nothing else to give because I gave Him my life."

I said, "I like how you took the initiative and went forward and proclaimed the name of the Lord, but I must say this to you. Is there a part of you that is not aware of it, that you've left out of your relationship with God? Think about it. Sometimes, you cannot tell that you are holding some part of you back from God."

Jackie said, "I gave up my all. There is nothing else to give."

I assured Jackie, "I am not questioning your integrity or the commitment that you make with God. I was just wondering if there is a part of you that is fighting against the Spirit, and you are not aware of it. This is very hard for me to say, but that will stop your relationship with God. Sometimes, it is hard to tell, but living in this world can let you do things out of the will of God. I am here to remind you there is nothing in your life that is important more than the love of God.

"When you make a commitment to God, He will always be there for you. Your life will never be the same. Take, for instance, when you are in a relationship with God, you can bring all your problems, the aspects of your heart, personality, and your emotions to him, and He will work on them. Isaiah 41:10 (NIV) says, 'So do not fear, for I am with you; do not be dismayed, for I am your God. I will strengthen you and help you; I will uphold you with my righteous right hand.'"

Jackie did not grasp what I was trying to tell her about the part of herself that was left behind, so I offered this illustration: "Suppose you have a back pain that doesn't go away, but you see a doctor who diagnoses you with pinched nerves and puts you on medication. Unfortunately, you forgot to tell him you're allergic to some medication. Even with the right medication, you still have the back pain."

She said, "Yes."

"I think you did not make yourself clear with the doctor because you should have told him your job description and why your pain is not going away."

Jackie's job required lifting, and that increased the pain in her back.

Sometimes, when we pray to God, we hold back on our prayer because we refuse to tell God everything, but God knows everything. In order for us to get our blessing, we must be true to ourselves.

Jackie was holding back because she was trying to win her daughter's love, and at the same time, she was putting herself in a bad spot. By talking to her, I noticed she was afraid. One lady from the usher team asked her if she was afraid to be alone or if she told her daughter the truth. She was also afraid of being more open with other people about how difficult things really were, perhaps, because she thought they would see her as an unfit mother. The usher team counseled her, "You do not have to be afraid. God will never let anyone take your daughter away from you."

Most parents open the door of fear in their lives for more than one reason, but when you are in a relationship with God, you cannot bring fear into that relationship. I told her, "I think you genuinely love God, and the only fear you should fear is the fear of God; just that would be a good place to start."

Jackie did some thinking about what the usher team said. She told the usher team, "Now, everything starts to open up to me after I have read what the Bible says about fear."

Joshua 1:9 (NIV) says, "Have I not commanded you? Be strong and courageous. Do not be afraid; do not be discouraged, for the LORD your God will be with you wherever you go."

Jackie told them, "I was so afraid. I thought it was a sign of weakness or a lack of trust." She also said, "I had been afraid to be afraid, so to speak."

Jackie reached a turning point in her life. She began facing her fears. In the same progress, she prayed and asked God for help with them. She talked to the usher team, who helped her deal with them. As time went by, her life began changing, as she became less afraid to do what it took to help her daughter go forward in life. God took her fear and gave her something much better.

God gave her the love of His Son, the One who came and died for you and me, and today we can say we have the victory over all demons. The love of the Lord is so precious. Jackie came to realize that the love of the Lord brought her to a point in her life where she could say, "I love You, Lord, with all my heart."

Matthew 22:37-38 (NIV) tells us that the greatest love of all is the first commandment: "Love the Lord your God with all your heart and with all your soul and with all your mind."

Deuteronomy 6:5 tells us that the love of God is the greatest command because it serves as an all-encompassing principle that covers all the other rules of life. It helps us live in this world and understand the Word of the Lord more and more every day. If we love Him, we must show our love for Him by going out in the world and proclaiming His Word. If we follow His way, He will always be there for us: "And he said to them, 'Go into all the world and proclaim the gospel to the whole creation'" (Mark 16:15, ESV). In fact, in Matthew 22:37-40 (ESV), Jesus enforced two of the laws:

> You shall love the Lord your God with all your heart
> and with all your soul and with all your mind. This
> is the great and first commandment. And a second
> is like it: You shall love your neighbor as yourself.

There is a time coming that we must live by these laws. It will help us engage in a relationship with the Lord.

There are so many bad things going on in the world today. For the few Christians that are praying, God looks into their prayers and answers them. There is a time coming, a set time, of which the Lord said, "Enough is enough. I am coming for My sheep." We have all heard that before the Lord's coming, some people will die before they see His coming. I am here to remind you that the Lord has a set time for Him to come and take over this world. Acts 17:31 (KJV) says,

> Because he hath appointed a day, in the which he
> will judge the world in righteousness by that man
> whom he hath ordained; whereof he hath given as-
> surance unto all men, in that he hath raised him
> from the dead.

After the church prayed with Jackie, they told her that was a second coming of the Lord. The pastor told Jackie, "Please do not wait until a bad situation comes up in your life again before you surrender your life to the Lord." Two weeks later, Jackie was baptized and started attending our Sunday school. She was active in the church; six months later, she got married. She visited churches and encouraged ladies regarding how to deal with problems in their lives. This is all about a set time in your life that God places for you; nothing can happen before that appointed time.

LET GOD VIEW YOUR LIFE

There are ways that someone in this world can try to view your life, but let God view it because man is an earthly being and can make mistakes. Here is a brief list of some of the most important aspects in which God abides. Some of these words can help you stay stronger in God because there is a time coming when no one can stop you, so be strong and courageous.

When you and I abide in the Lord, we have to tolerate some things that people have done to us. If we endure all those things and stay on the cross, we will get a star in our crown. First Samuel 1:22 says, "But Hannah went not up; for she said unto her husband, I will not go up until the child be weaned, and then I will bring him, that he may appear before the LORD, and there abide for ever." Hannah acted in accordance with her wish. The Lord established His Word, so the woman abode and weaned her son.

Day after day, we cry to God about things we need. We should take a look around us and look at the overflow, the increase, and the growth. Sometimes, when we work with pastors, we receive no cash, but we labor for love in our Lord Jesus Christ. First Thessalonians 3:12 (KJV) says, "And the Lord make you to increase and abound in love one toward another, and toward all men, even as we do toward you." Some of us do not know how much they are valued. Christ went on the cross and died for them, so we must follow Him because He is the most important thing in our life.

The soul is the spiritual part of a person that some people believe continues to exist in some form after their body has died (Cambridge Dictionary). The soul is also the part of a person or thing that expresses the basic qualities that make it what it is. It is the principle of life, feeling, thought, and action in humans, regarded as a distinct entity separate from the body and commonly held to be separable in existence from the body (Dictionary.com, LLC).

KEEP YOUR FAITH
UNTIL THE RIGHT TIME

Ultimately, loving God is about keeping the faith. It is supposed to be a complete bond in which all of us are connected to everything God makes available in His kingdom. When you think about God and what He has done for you, it makes your life worth living. Some people think that loving God is difficult because you cannot see Him. When you love with every fiber of your being, that is what matters to Him. If you let God know your secrets, fears, and deepest desires, He will help you. God took the risks of the vulnerability and opened the door in your life.

Some people, who have experienced this type of bond with God, will tell you that this sort of deep and full relationship makes them feel good inside. Life is good. It is good and has meaning. Some people say things like, "I can remember when all people saw was black and white, but now the whole world is full of color." For instance, when you tell someone that you love them with the love of God, you are painting a picture of how God wants us to love Him: with all our hearts.

To engage in the Word of God in all the ways that are possible is a lifelong and safe journey. In reality, the more aspects of our lives and soul we can bring to Him, the more able God is to make a set time in your life, a time that no one can change; God's purposes are ahead of you. It can be anything: your growth and efficacy in using your talents and gifts, success at work, or service to others. At the same time, loving God is easy as long as we use all of our inner being to unlock the door of struggles in our lives, like heartbreaking problems with children and bad habits.

The truth is God will make time in your life that no one can change, and that is a set time, that time ordained from the beginning of time for you to go forward in life. That is what trusting Him completely is all about. It can get the card from around your neck. He tells them, "Take a part of Me that you need." Jesus loves God completely; Matthew 22:37 (NIV) tells us that Jesus replied, "Love the Lord your God with all your heart and with all your soul and with all your mind." When we love God with all of ourselves, He has access to help and illuminates us, and we have the opportunity to go forward in life.

The door of life is open to us when we are connected to the love of God. When we are not connected to Him, we are living a life with no hope. We must have hope in God because the time we live in is full of troubles. The stock market falls, and people lose their jobs: the future is uncertain. We, as Christians, have hope. We have someone to cry to because the Lord told us that He will never leave us or forsake us. For instance, in today's economy, there is little to no hope for the future; however, God is never surprised. Some people think there is no hope. Even some biblical heroes had their time when they wanted to give up. This includes men like Moses, Jonah, Job, and Jeremiah, even some powerful prophets in the Old Testament, like Elijah.

The world's definitions of hope are different from God's. Some people might hope their Super Bowl team wins. Some hope that they never lose their jobs or their house. The hope we have in God is more certain than the sun rising in the morning. Psalm 119:74 (NIV) says, "I have put my hope in your word."

Some people have real hope. For example, when a person reads the Word of God, they can know for certain that they have a secure and certain future with God. He will never allow us to suffer beyond our imagination or give us more than we can handle. People try so many things on this earth, and they fail, but to be more certain, they have hope in God, in Christ.

Psalm 130:7 (NIV) says, "Put your hope in the LORD, for with the LORD is unfailing love and with him is full redemption." God wanted believers to know that when they rest assured in Him, His love is unfailing. God will never drive His believers in days of calamity. He has rescued the born-again believers for a special time. He made a promise to us that if we keep the faith, we will have an eternal home with Him.

When we have hope, we earn the gift that was promised to us in Ephesians 1:13 (NIV), which says, "And you also were included in Christ when you heard the message of truth, the gospel of your salvation. When you believed, you were marked in him with a seal, the promised Holy Spirit." God is truth, and when we hear the truth, we put our trust in Him, and He gives us the Holy Spirit to seal us as we engage in His Word. For our future of hope is in Him. Jeremiah 29:11 says, "'For I know the plans I have for you declares,' the LORD, 'plans to prosper you and not to harm you, plans to give you hope and a future.'" God has plans for us if we just stay with Him. Some of us have plans for our children, but the plans that God has for us are bigger. His plans are not intended to harm us; His plans are to elevate us. This does not mean that you may be a millionaire, but your future is well secure. The plan that God has for us is unknown to the human mind; He said, "Even if you do not know, I promised to take care of My children." Your insurance broker and financial adviser might have plans for your future. They tried to put money aside to secure your future, but in the long run, they failed. They do not have the ability to let it happen. God holds the future, and He plans it better than anyone else can.

What is hope? It is for today, tomorrow, and an expectation for things to happen. Psalm 131:3 (NIV) says, "Put your hope in the LORD both now and forevermore." Jesus makes it clear to all Christians that He will never leave us, never forsake us, and will never ever cast us away (John 6:37). He made this promise; it is for today, tomorrow, next week, and the years to come. This promise is for believers to stay on the firing line because a time is coming that no one can stop you, and that is a set time. When you develop the spirit of hope, it will stay with you until Jesus comes for us.

Your marriage failed, love for your children failed, love for boss failed, and love for your family failed, but God's love will never fail. When you put your loving hope in the Lord Jesus Christ, He is your Father, your grandfather, and you are His children. When you have a problem, He is there to give you advice and offer the hope that everything will work out for you despite what today may seem like. Romans 8:28 (KJV) says, "And we know that all things work together for good to them that love God, to them who are the called according to his purpose." So, too, does the Lord delight when we put our hope in Him and His unfailing love. He wants us to depend upon Him for everything. Psalm 37:4 (KJV) says, "Delight thyself also in the LORD; and he shall give thee the desires of thine heart."

Brother and sister, when you put your hope in the true and living God, never be ashamed. Psalm 25:3 tells us no one whose hope is in God will ever be put to shame. The children of God put their hope in the right place, and not in themselves, their jobs, or in their circumstances that will distract them from the love of God. You will never be disappointed or ashamed when you place your hope in Him because He has the power to deliver us out of all our problems. Power was given to Him. Some people think that their pension and their social security have such power. God made this whole earth. He owns every animal in the forest, and He is the owner of the cattle on thousand hills. Psalm 50:10-11 (NIV) says, "For every animal of the forest is mine, and the cattle on a thousand hills. I know every bird in the mountains, and the insects in the fields are mine."

God put a special emphasis on the animals, and we are higher than the animal. He will guide us through this sinful world. We, as human beings, have the privilege to put our hope in Him because we are the highest class of animals. Psalm 25:5 (NIV) says, "Guide me in your truth and teach me, for you are God my Savior, and my hope is in you all day long."

We are just human beings created in Your likeness and cannot look beyond today, but You are God, and You have a plan for every step that we take.

We have hope in You, and we pray that You will guide us and protect us even in areas where the dark shadows of death seem imminent in the most dangerous place (Psalm 23). We might plan our own course, but God Himself determines where our steps go (Proverbs 16:9).

When we step out in this world, we must be courageous and have hope because the Lord God is with us. However, if we are not believers, the hope we have is in this world and among men; we are so miserable. As children of God, we can take heart and be strong and courageous because God is our hope. When God is your hope, the enemy will try to conquer you, but when God is the boat, you can smile at the storm. Psalm 31:24 (NIV) tells us to "Be strong and take heart, all you who hope in the Lord."

We can be in this world, but we are not a part of this world. If we are a part of this world, we are consumed with worry because we don't know what comes next. We must put all our hope in God because He is the One who can guarantee our future. If God holds the future, we should give Him reverence. We must not be afraid because the Lord is good. His mercy is everlasting, and His hope is to all generations. According to Psalm 33:18 (NIV), "But the eyes of the Lord are on those who fear him, on those whose hope is in his unfailing love." When reading the Bible and seeing the word "fear," we must not be afraid because that fear is not a fear of punishment or retribution. This fear is awesome and is about giving reverential respect and standing in awe before God. This is what fear of the true and living God means. It means that those who revere God and His name have nothing to fear at all: no evil, no pestilence, no begging for bread, and no fear of want. His unfailing love is upon those that fear or revere Him; His love never fails, and His eyes are fixed on them in a permanent gaze that is transfixed upon their today and tomorrow. They are the apple of His eye (Deuteronomy 32:10; Zechariah 2:8).

He will never leave you or forsake you because you are the apple of His eye. He will protect you. Psalm 33:20 (NIV) says, "We wait in hope for the Lord; He is our help and our shield." He is our going out and our coming in. His hope is a shield to our life. His hope is a shield to eternal, present, and past lives. When we call up His name, He is a shield when we need protecting. What a mighty God we serve; He alone is our help and our shield.

If you are not a born-again Christian, then you have no hope in this lifetime. Your future is not good, and you have no idea what will come next. Some people are good at loving the hope in God with their head but not with their heart. They are good: working in the church, helping people, and knowing what's right and prudent to do, but after the hope in their heart runs down, they give up. Some of them have strong emotions that are hard to control; no matter what their brain tells them to do, they do the opposite. This is one set of people who struggle with an impulsive attitude. Their heart is not working well with the rest of their body. When these individuals begin unleashing God's love and hope into their heart and opening up to Him, their head and heart begin to work together and put things in the right perspective. This makes perfect sense because God does things in accordance with His holy, divine nature, which is consistent with His will (Genesis 18:14; 42:1-2). This is right. He is never in conflict with Himself. Because we are connected to God, we experience fewer problems in our life.

Psalm 33:18 (NIV) says, "But the eyes of Lord are on those who fear him, on those whose hope is in his unfailing love." When we suffer from emotional pain, relationship stress, problems, and faith struggles, God sets a time in our lives to change all those things. There is no clearer indication of how God will set a time in your life, and no one can change it. By nature, God is a God of love and hope. Psalm 9:18 (NASB) says, "For the needy will not always be forgotten, Nor the hope of the afflicted perish forever." I encourage you to receive Jesus Christ as your personal Lord and savior today. Tomorrow is promised to no one. Do it right now, and you have the assurance of hope in God for today, tomorrow, and for all eternity.

There are times when we get sick. We go to the doctor. He gives us different types of medication, but nothing works. One day, we pray to God for His healing power, and it starts to work to the extent that we bring all of our inner parts to Him. Many people have experienced the loss of a significant long-term partner. For instance, someone you love deeply is no longer in your life. We try to pray over it, get over it, think positively, and do all sorts of things to get something so bad and painful out of our mind. It is so bad that the intent feeling of grief still remains. Sometimes, we have to pray and allow God to give us hope that we find someone that will fulfill those same needs. Sometimes, it is not easy to replace the one you have been in love with for a long time. It is not that you are afraid to be close again. It is not easy just to go out and have fun. At times, you have to ask God to help you to get close to someone again in your life. It will come to the point that you will realize that only God can heal the human body. You must also understand that God will go to the extremes to love you and have you connected with Him again. At the same time, you and I have a role to play. Put away all our needs and love God with all your heart. If we stand on the premise of God, He will send the right person or the right people in our lives to elevate us to the next level in life. It is as the Bible teaches in Psalm 119:74 (NIV), "May those who fear you rejoice when they see me, for I have put my hope in your word."

What the Love of God Does

He gave up His one and only Son. God is about love. John 3:16 (ESV) says, "For God so loved the world, that he gave his only Son, that whoever believes in him should not perish but have eternal life." God makes the time for His people that love Him with everything they have, with every fiber of their being. It is not hard to understand: the more of yourself you give to God, the more of Himself He makes available to you. When you pray, just wait on God because your time is not God's time. Second Peter 3:8 (KJV) says, "But, beloved, be not ignorant of this one thing, that one day is with the Lord as a thousand years, and a thousand years as one day."

Whatever obstacle or setback you are facing, take it to God in prayer. There is nothing too hard for God to do. If he can part the Red Sea, open the eyes of the blind, and make the lame walk, the psalmist says He will do it for you. He does not know how or when, but He will do it. When you have the ability to love God, love Him with every part of your body, heart, soul, and mind, and watch the real miracles start to work in your life. It was on a Monday morning when Nicolas was going to work. He dropped the kids at school. The next stop was to drop his wife at work. Unfortunately, the car came to a sudden stop in the middle of the road. Here came a truck, hit the car; thank God, no one was hurt. Psalm 27:5 (KJV) says, "For in the time of trouble He shall hide me in his pavilion: in the secret of His tabernacle shall he hide me; he shall set me upon a rock."

The devil will try to hurt God's people, but the love of God will keep them. Luke 22:31 (KJV) says, "And the Lord said, Simon, Simon, behold, Satan hath desired to have you, that he may sift you as wheat." The devil attacked God's people because he dislikes the Lord. God told us when the evil one is coming to attack us, He will send His holy angel to protect us. Our God is still alive; He will never let something happen to you. When you leave your house and are at work, God is working behind everything. You do not know how many accidents God prevented you from. Even when Jonah disobeyed God, He sent Jonah help. Jonah 1:17 (KJV) says, "Now the Lord had prepared a great fish to swallow up Jonah. And Jonah was in the belly of the fish three days and three nights." We serve a big God. He knows when you are hungry. He knows how many hair on your head. Deuteronomy 10:17 (KJV) says, "For the Lord your God is God of gods, and Lord of Lords, a great God, a mighty, and a terrible, which regarded not persons nor taketh reward."

Dating in a New Relationship

I was in a counseling class when a young man raised his hand and asked a question, "How can we know when God is talking to us? There is a problem."

"Something happened, and you thought you heard God speak to you?"

The young man said, "Yes, because when it was time for bed, I prayed. As I finished, I was wondering if God was trying to tell me that I should go back to my old girlfriend."

"Why did you come to that conclusion?" I asked.

"Well, when I was in church, I ran into her when I was going to pray at the altar. It came to my mind that God is telling me I should get back together with her."

I thought about it and said to myself, "I hope this young man is not drunk."

"What could have made you think that? Because you have run into her at the altar, you think that God is telling you to get back together with her?" I looked at him and shook my head. "Are you okay? I do not know how much you have to drink before you come to the church."

He looked at me and said, "What is that about?"

First, I said this, "The church is a public place, and if you run into someone that you were friends with, it does not mean that God is telling you to have a relationship with that person. People run into old friends every day, so if you think this is a sign that, if you got back together, it would be really good and nice, really good, you are making a mistake. If you do not pray about those things, you will end up with a broken heart and a bad dream. Philippians 4:6 (KJV) says, 'Be careful for nothing; but in every thing by prayer and supplication with thanksgiving let your requests be made know unto God.'

"Dating requires the Lord's attention. If you see someone that you think you could make life with, you should go to God in prayer. Remember, He is your father, and He will give you the blessing to go forward. Psalm 55:22 (KJV) says, 'Cast thy burden upon the Lord, and He shall sustain thee: he shall never suffer the righteous to be moved.'"

I asked the young man about this lady, "How did she treat you? I just want to make sure that you are doing the right thing. The last time when you were with her, what happened? What was the relationship like? Was it good?" I asked.

"No," he said, "it was bad. She made me feel inferior. She did not treat me well. It was like a nightmare."

"Well then," I said, "I would look into your problem and see how I can help you. At the same time, I hope that she thinks about you the same way you think about her. It sounds like you guys should take it one day at a time, clean up your act, and make the right decision. Psalm 37:4 (KJV) says, 'Delight thyself also in the Lord; and He shall give thee the desires of thine heart.'" I told him, "This was not a sign from God at all."

He looked at me with a sad face.

I said afterward, "I think my response was a little hard on him." I also said, "Some people take whatever comes their way and hope that God will change the person in the relationship. God will help you, but at the same time, you have to make a good decision as a human being."

Psalm 25:4-5 (KJV) says, "Show me thy ways, O Lord; teach me thy paths. Lead me in thy truth, and teach me; for thou art the God of my salvation; on thee do I wait all the day."

Getting Ready to Date

Many people make poor decisions when it comes to dating. It is very important to know something about the person you are dating. Dating out of the will of God can be difficult. First John 2:16 (KJV) says, "For all that is in the world, the lust of the flesh, and the lust of eyes, and the pride of life, is not of the Father, but is of the world." I think Christians should date Christians because dating someone who is not a Christian can cause a problem. Take, for instance, when it is time to attend church: that person who is not a churchgoer may be just coming home from a party. The person who is not a Christian does things that are different from a Christian person: sometimes, he or she wants to drink alcohol and smoke a cigarette. Sometimes, the person who is not a Christian tries to stop the Christian from going to church meetings and curses them about their God. Christians must be careful who they are attracted to. Matthew 6:33 (KJV) says, "But seek ye first the kingdom of God, and His righteousness; and all these things shall be added unto you."

Remember: God takes care of His people; He will never disappoint you. He takes care of the bird of the air. When the right time comes, God will send the right person into your life. James 4:10 (ESV) says, "Humble yourselves before the Lord, and He will exalt you." The question is: why is it that we're just naturally attracted to some people and not to others?

Dating can sometimes be a problem. That's the reason some people give up on dating altogether. Sometimes, you can become disillusioned and lose interest in dating. Many pastors preach and teach that God does not want you to date. It may sound that way, but dating is a beautiful thing and a good way to start a relationship. Dating can also be a time of learning, fun, growth, and a nice time of human interaction as one gets ready to start a relationship. Dating is amazing, but sometimes it can be dangerous if you are dating the wrong person. Second Corinthians 6:14 (KJV) says, "Be ye not unequally yoked together with unbelievers: for what fellowship hath righteousness with unrighteousness? and what communion hath light with darkness?"

We are so quick to say, "I believe the Lord has given me this person." We must be sure and consult the Lord in prayer. Take the time and listen to His conviction and stop doing what you want to do because if the person is not a Christian, then God did not give that person to you. If you are planning to enter into a relationship with an unbeliever, you are wrong; you will make the biggest mistake in your life. Take the time and date and learn about the person because if that person claims to be a Christian but lives like an unbeliever, God didn't send you that person. My God will never send you a fake Christian to marry you. Proverbs 18:22 (KJV) says, "Whoso findeth a wife findeth a good thing, and obtaineth favour of the LORD."

Many people believe that they are in love for reasons such as the person's looks, communication skills, etc. Did you talk to God about that person? Do you believe that God sent that person in your life for you to get married? Falling in love can be dangerous. It is not up to you; pray about it, and God will send the right person. True love is built on actions, choices, and Christ as the mediator. Most of all, that person has to prove himself or herself over time because many married went into divorce and caused family problems. There are so many things in this world that can make you deceived. It is important to ask God to send the right person your way, and you will not date for fun or for a good time or to impress people. God wants His children to have a Christian marriage full of fun. When it comes to marriage, it must be the greatest tool in the life of the believer. Ecclesiastes 9:9 (KJV) says,

Live joyfully with the wife whom thou lovest all the days of the life of thy vanity, which he hath given thee under the sun, all the days of thy vanity: for that is thy portion in this life, and in thy labour which thou takest under the sun.

Sanctification of Marriage

God instituted marriage to His people on the earth. It is the most significant relationship anyone could ever have. Ephesians 5:25-26 (KJV) says, "Husbands, love your wives, even as Christ also loved the church, and gave himself for it; That he might sanctify and cleanse it with the washing of water by the word." In order for you to have a good marriage, you have to trust God. The Word of God states that "marriage should be honored by all, and the marriage bed kept pure, for God will judge the adulterer and all the sexually immoral" (Hebrews 13:4, NIV). In 1 Corinthians 7:1-9 (NIV), Paul wrote,

> Now for the matters you wrote about: "It is good for a man not to have sexual relations with a woman." But since sexual immorality is occurring, each man should have sexual relations with his own wife, and each woman with her own husband. The husband should fulfill his marital duty to his wife, and likewise the wife to her husband. The wife does not have authority over her own body but yields it to her husband. In the same way, the husband does not have authority over his own body but yields it to his wife.

Everyone should study the Bible because if we follow the Word of God, the whole world would be a better place to live. Sex and money cause problems in many relationships.

Sex is a wonderful gift when it is expressed within the marriage covenant.

Do not deprive each other except perhaps by mutual consent and for a time, so that you may devote yourselves to prayer. Then come together again so that Satan will not tempt you because of your lack of self-control. I say this as a concession, not as a command. I wish that all of you were as I am. But each of you has your own gift from God: one has this gift, another has that. Now to the unmarried and the widows I say: It is good for them to stay unmarried, as I do. But if they cannot control themselves, they should marry, for it is better to marry than to burn with passion.

1 Corinthians 7:5-9 (NIV)

Burning with passion can be dangerous because some people live outside the will of God to have sex. It may sound good at first, but after a while, there are consequences. There are often physical consequences, such as unwanted pregnancy or sexually transmitted diseases.

What Is the Strength
of a Good Marriage?

My pastor always asks the couples in my church who have long-lasting marriages what the secret is. They will all turn and look at each other and say a thousand things like love, respect, "let the wife win all the time," and "remember that marriage did not come from heaven; it was ordained on the earth, so it needs more time to work on."

Some people think they have the key to a good marriage; it is not sex. Sometimes, you have to act on emptying yourself to keep the marriage going. Marriage is an investment. In order for you to build a sustaining marriage, you have to bring all of your parts into it. Every married couple should love each other the same way that we are to love God: with all our heart, soul, mind, and strength (Mark 12:30). Some people who are truly in a marriage know and understand that some marriages take more time than others to get adjusted. These are some things that would develop only because of the union of two people that have faith to go forward in life. Do what God says in His Word about a married couple. Ephesians 4:2-3 (ESV) says, "With all humility and gentleness, with patience, bearing with one another in love, eager to maintain the unity of the Spirit in the bond of peace."

However, marriage is not a tightrope. It is more like a commitment that involves agreeing to fulfill a covenant to your spouse in the eyes of God. Some people are committed to their marriage, but sometimes, it is up, and sometimes it is down, but their hearts are in the right place. There is another group of married couples that struggle and feel empty inside. Marriage is a give-and-take relationship. Remember: the person you are married to is not perfect; it will take hard work to understand each other. Every individual that engages in marriage will experience some problems, so have a genuine heart because sometimes, the road can be rocky.

We need to approach marriage with all of our strong passions and promises and ask God to guide us. We all ask God for a good marriage, yet some people think they can make a good marriage. Some of them start out very good, but when fear and weakness come in, they lose their hope and dreams; they start to struggle and become disappointed in the situation. If you are of the kind, my heart goes out to you. Sometimes, a situation like this can be a sign from God. He is trying to bring you close to Him because, in order for your marriage to work out, you first have to seek the face of God. 1 John 4:7 (KJV) says, "Beloved, let us love one another; for love is of God; and every one that loveth is born of God, and knoweth God."

Sometimes, marriage problems can push people for the first time in their lives, and then they start to look back into their lives and question themselves because they have encountered something that is bigger than them. They look to God for the answer, and at the same time, some of those people never go to church or give God the praise. In marriage, as in every area of life, problems will come, but if you trust God, there is a time coming that no man can stop you, and that is a set time when God will work out His blessings upon your life. Do not lose hope because there is nothing that is impossible for God (Luke 1:37). Pray over your marriage; tell God the problem, and He will fix it for you. It is not that the plans of couples for their marriage do not work, but the evil one tries to discourage the first marriage. Sometimes, you cannot imagine where the problems will come from, but as a couple, you are experiencing some serious problems. God has placed two of you together, and with His supernatural power, He will take care of your marriage. Mark 10:9 (BSB) says, "Therefore what God has joined together, let man not separate."

THE FORMAT OF A GODLY MARRIAGE

The people who make cars have a certain way or system of making the cars. Many companies have a way of doing things, so you can distinguish their cars from other companies. A basketball player has a signature move; no one can use it. This is the same with a good marriage. A good marriage must have beliefs, values, and influences that God placed in it for you to follow. Genesis 2:24 presents the format for a good marriage, which is one man and one woman united together to become one flesh: therefore a man shall leave his father and his mother and hold fast to his wife, and they shall become one flesh. Many cultures shape marriages and conduct them in different ways and systems. It is not supposed to be that way. Christian marriage should not be shaped by culture. A good marriage must be built on the foundation of the cross of Jesus Christ and the Word of God. When Christians come together in marriage, they dare not allow the world or our culture to shape our thinking, our attitudes, or our actions. The purpose of this is to consider Christian marriage primarily in the light of God.

When it comes to Christian marriage, if one of the partners is a believer in Christ who embraces the attitudes and the actions that are prescribed by God, when a problem sets in, He will show up. Some people think that in a Christian marriage, the two partners must be Christians; that is the right way, but if one is a Christian, God can still manifest Himself through the marriage relationship through at least one of them. First Peter 3:1-6 says that a believer's wife may manifest Christ while married to an unbeliever, so you and I must not call this marriage any less than Christian marriage.

At the same time, we, as Christians who are married, must act like children of God. Our action must flow from the Scriptures; we must not be governed by the same principles that guide the secular marriage in the world. Christian marriages do not just happen naturally: they happen unnaturally. We have to wait on the supernatural as we obey the Scriptures and depend upon the grace of God.

As a married couple, you should have God in the center of your marriage all the time. He is the One who ordained marriage on the earth, so we must invite God into our relationship so that we can go to Him for guidance and direction about our marriage. Due to the fact that God is the author of the institution of marriage and the creator of souls, He does what He wants to do because He is God, and He knows what is good for you as a friend and a married couple. He has set a time in your life that no one can change. Put your marriage and your life into His hands, and He will see you through. He commanded us to obey all these things and to fear the Lord our God so that we might always keep the faith.

As a married couple, you must invest your time and energy in your marriage and work even harder on your relationship, and God will be there with you. If God is in your investment, it will grow because He says in Matthew 6:21 (NIV), "For where your treasure is, there your heart will be also." Your heart is the center of your marriage. No matter how good your marriage is, it can be better. A good marriage is in the hands of God, but there are some important qualities that should be incorporated. Both partners have to pray hard, commit to the relationship, and invest their time and energy into it. Sometimes, they need to take time out to communicate effectively with each other and know how to resolve their differences. Work hard; play hard; learn to be flexible in your marriage because there is no right way or wrong way to keep a marriage. Let God be in the center of it.

Some people think a relationship is only good if it comes easily. Most good relationships take a lot of hard work, prayer, and investment. Daily communication is the key to a good marriage. At the same time, it is important to be truthful, honest, and strong, and that will also help your marriage. A truthful marriage will help you invest more in the relationship, but dishonesty and deception cause division in the relationship. Marriage is a two-way street. In order for you to get to your destination, both of you have to walk on that street.

SEX AND MARRIAGE GO TOGETHER

In the eyes of God, sex is a gift. When God put a man and a woman in the garden, He had a plan. God created sex for reproduction for us to make babies; He also created it for intimacy, for our pleasure. The Bible tells us that Christians can't engage in sex like the world.

God designed sex for a husband and wife to express their love to one another. If someone talks about sex in a larger audience like a church, people look at them like they are saying something bad, but at the same time, 99 percent of the people in the world are having sex. In a ladies' retreat at a church, a minister came from out of town and told the ladies to spend quality time with their husbands. Most Christians are so busy they can't find the time for their loved ones, and that creates problems in the relationship. It is good to help in the church; working with God is good, but at the same time, you are dishonoring your spouse. "However, each one of you also must love his wife as he loves himself, and the wife must respect her husband" (Ephesians 5:33, NIV).

Sexual awareness has always existed; it is always in the nature and heart of God. Sex is the gift from God; it is deeply rooted in the relationship as God is. We are sexual beings; sex is the satisfying intimate part of life. It is built on the foundation of God. Sex is also an emotional connection between a wife and a husband. It is true some people say the greater the relationship is, the better the sex is. Take, for instance, when a husband's eyes meet his wife's during sex: it is a dream come true.

Christians do not approach intimacy the way the world does. They go by the Bible, so it takes a little time, but when the time is right and God is in it, the waiting makes it better. The love and promises that God gave us should be forever cherished. When a husband and a wife get together and call upon the name of the Lord, it is like shining a light into a dark place. 1 Corinthian 7:2 (KJV) says, "Nevertheless, to avoid fornication, let every man have his own wife, and let every woman have her own husband."

Some people abuse sex. Some people do not know the truly fundamental, essential nature of sex. Christian must take a different approach. Christians should pray before engaging in sex. Read the Bible, and it will help you; sex is a mystery we cannot fully understand. We may know a great deal about the way it comes and why God put it here, but at the same time, the mystery of the attraction is still unknown. Many people wrote books and told stories about sex in their own words, but none of them can compare to Solomon. In Song of Solomon 7:8 (NIV), it says, "'I will climb the palm tree: I will take hold of its fruit.' May your breasts be like clusters of grapes on the vine, the fragrance of your breath like apples." Solomon's words help us get ourselves into the sexual act itself with tenderness, passion, and all the energy.

It is the plan of God for two people to become one. It also brings that sexual energy to two people who are individuals and merged their lives into one. The Bible tells us that a marriage relationship is a good thing. Genesis 2:24 (ESV) says, "Therefore a man shall leave his father and his mother and hold fast to his wife, and they shall become one flesh." When two people enter into God's covenant, sexual intercourse is legal for them. They can experience the emotional merger that a married couple has when they come together. Married couples must keep the fire burning. Research tells us that people who are married for a long time still have an active sexual life compared to people who are married for a shorter time. It is sad to say some couples' sex life is dying out because of so many things like work, money, and family problems.

Sexual attraction is common around the world today, but people refuse to take the right step to engage in it. Some people think that just going to bed is all people must do to connect at the sexual level in their life. The difference between those people and Christians is they make their relationship with one man or one woman in their lives. Sex helps us understand God's full design. It also lets us experience something larger than ourselves, so if you are a Christian, do not be afraid to have sexual intercourse with your husband or your wife. Psalm 139:14 (NIV) says we have truly been "fearfully and wonderfully made."

People have been saying for the past years that there is a problem; sometimes, when it comes to sex, it mostly affects men. Researchers say some medications cause a problem to some man's sexual lifestyle. Take, for instance, sickness like high blood pressure and diabetes, just to name a few. Some wives feel like their husband is not attracted to them sexually, so they feel like it is a loss of interest, but it is more than that. A couple can be physically healthy and active, but when it comes to sex, they lose interest in it because of different reasons.

In other words, it should not matter. It is good to have a sexual relationship, but if there is a problem with one member of the couple, that should not stop the relationship. You should remember the institution of marriage and the love in your heart for that person and leave it in the hands of God. At the same time, take some classes about sexual intimacy and learn some techniques that can help you keep your relationship going. You were born a sexual being, so it is hard for sexuality to get disconnected from your heart. When a couple gets together and there are mixed feelings in their heart, it will manifest in their sex. In addition, some men abuse sex that God gave to them. A man has the capacity for fathering multiple children with multiple women at the same time. It is sad to say that some men take that opportunity and mess up the life of many ladies. Men must come to their senses. Just because there is no expiration period on their reproductive capability, that does not give them the right to get multiple women pregnant. A man can father children until he dies; as long as he does not have any physical abnormalities or surgeries, he has the capacity for reproduction.

When putting all this together, we can see that God only wants children to be produced between a man and a woman within the confines of marriage. We can see that God wanted sex only to occur within marriage. God can do all things, so He created marriage with sex. In Ephesians 5, God tells us He created marriage as a symbol of the relationship between Christ and the church. We can truly say God is marvelous; He designed the church as a symbol of His love for us. In Psalm 45, a prophetic song about Jesus Christ, we see how He desires the beauty of His church.

People Murmuring
with Attitude

When I was twenty-six years of age, I attended a church in the Bronx, NY. The pastor was a good man. He made sure everything was well with the members. One day, my church sister by the name of Ashley came up to me and asked a question, "Why are these people murmuring like that?" She said something to me that caught me off guard, and as I was going through all the possible things I could say, an answer came to mind, so in response, I asked, "Why would you say that?"

"Ashley," she said.

"Why would the pastor want to deal with murmuring people?"

"What do you mean 'Ashley'? So I say because he has to!"

"Why does he have to?" Ashley? Asked further.

I thought for a moment. I know that we all run into difficult people and that sometimes, we have to deal with them. I laughed because of the way she asked the question. It made me think that she was looking for an answer that she could use to say to the pastor.

Then, she looked at me and said, "Sorry, because they're everywhere!" I could not help but laugh. I looked at her because she sounded like she talked about the Israelites that Moses took from Egypt. My response was, "They are not everywhere." If she truly were encountering them everywhere, her experience wasn't normal. It came to my mind that she might have a hand in why murmuring people kept appearing in her life.

I sat down to hear her; she started telling me about murmuring people at her job. She used to attend church with her family and friends. It looked like she found them just about everywhere she went. It looked like something was going on in her life. We talked for a moment. I could sense trouble. It was not hard to see no matter what situation she found herself in, this lady would somehow be one of the most difficult people to please, and she kept on talking about her group leader. It seemed like she always attracted murmuring people like a magnet, and at the same time, she tried to please all the people around her and was trying to live up to their expectations. I tried to tell her in the simplest way that I knew, "People will murmur and complain. Moses dealt with it, but all you have to do is pray for them and, at the same time, help them. Let those people know that you are there for them."

Okay, let's talk. Do you think this lady is taking the right approach, saying there is no escape from murmuring people? Do you think that they are everywhere? Do you think that my answer is appropriate and true? I think you should draw those murmuring people's attention to the Bible and let them read it. James 5:9 (BSB) says, "Do not complain about one another, brothers, so that you will not be judged." Tell them the truth from the Bible.

Some of the time, we find ourselves in a situation where we have to collaborate with murmuring people. The truth is we know that we are not helpless in dealing with them. Sometimes, we can play a part in attracting them into our lives. We must pray to God to help these people that murmur and complain that they may change and be forgiving and stand firm in the Lord. If these people murmur and complain, but if they stay in the Lord, there is hope for them. God will send someone to help those people. Isaiah 29:24 (KJV) says, "They also that erred in spirit shall come to understanding, and they that murmured shall learn doctrine."

The Bible tells us that people face a lot of situations in life. Some of them give up, and some of them pray for change. Sometimes, the change comes, but they do not accept it because it does not come the way they want it to come. Take, for instance, the Israelites who were in Egypt for years crying to God for help, so God sent them help. On their way from Egypt, the murmuring started against Moses and Aaron: "Wherefore hath the Lord brought us unto this land, to fall by the sword, that our wives and our children should be a prey? were it not better for us to return into Egypt?" (Numbers 14:3, KJV).

A SPIRITUAL LESSON

In my time of preaching, I have come in contact with some difficult people. A young man walked up to me one day and said, "I have a secret. It is so bad." He wanted to talk to someone about it, but something inside of him was saying, "If you were following the leading of the Holy Spirit, you would be more powerful in God's work. If you would be patient and have unconditional love for the people around you, you would feel the power of God in you, and a great miracle would take place."

Some people want God to bless them, but at the same time, they do not want to go through the problem that comes with life. Is life's problem so hard that you cannot stay in the presence of God? Is God good to you? The Bible tells us in Psalm 145:9 (KJV), "The LORD is good to all: and his tender mercies are over all his work."

If you believe in all these things, listen to the Word of God and give Him thanks. It was not the will of God for His people to go through hard times. God takes care of His people; sometimes, we do not deserve it, but what a mighty God we serve. In Matthew 6:26 (ESV), He says, "Look at the birds of the air: they neither sow nor reap nor gather into barns, and yet your heavenly Father feeds them." God told us to stop stressing about tomorrow, which we cannot even control nor do anything about.

People think that they can plan their day and make a schedule, but they have nothing to do with it. Luke 12:25 (NIV) says, "Who of you by worrying can add a single hour to your life?" God already planned your day for you; you are just going through the schedule. The way you plan it would make it hard to get things done; sometimes, you get so anxious like you can add hours to the day. He told us, "Do not worry and get anxious; it can shorten your lifespan." He made a promise to us in Genesis 28:15 (ESV), "I am with you […] wherever you go, and will bring you back to this land. For I will not leave you until I have done what I have promised you."

In fact, the way that God takes care of you, no human being on earth can ever repeat. He also sent His Son to die for us; what a mighty God we serve! Sometimes, when we pray, it looks like we get the things that we ask for; He also looks out for our personal interests and for the interests of others. Philippians 2:4) says that it is true that He takes care of us, so we must take a stand against the thing that people do and against the things that God warns us not to do. We must read the Bible and know the positive spiritual things that we can do. God's way is the right and best way to fight against bad things. Let today be the last day that you engage yourself in things that are not of God.

As Christ gave up His life for us, so we should be willing to lay down our lives for our brothers and sisters. We must transfer His love, responsibility, freedom, creativity, and redemption to the rest of the world. That has been His plan from the beginning. Jeremiah 29:11-12 (NIV) says,

> "For I know the plans I have for you," declares the LORD, "plans to prosper you and not to harm you, plans to give you hope and a future. Then you will call on me and come and pray to me, and I will listen to you."

God gave us everything on the earth so that we may live in good standing. Every child of God has a gift, but in order for that gift to operate, you have to help your brother and sister in God so that His love and grace may pass on. Remember Peter told us, "Each of you should use whatever gift you have received to help others, as faithful stewards of God's grace in its various forms" (1 Peter 4:10, NIV). All these gifts are for us so that we may appreciate the things of God and do not lust after the things of the world. One of the primary goals that God gives us these gifts is to equip us to glorify God. The spiritual gifts are for many purposes. They are "for the perfecting of the saints, for the work of the ministry, for the edifying of the body of Christ." We all must come together in faith and the knowledge of the Son of God (Ephesians 4:12-13).

First Corinthians 12 also tells us how God works in the believer to shape His perspective on life and motivate his work and actions. God gave wisdom, knowledge, faith, healing, working of miracles, prophecy, discerning of spirits, interpretation of tongues, "for as the body is one, and hath many members, and all the members of that one body, being many, are one body: so also is Christ" (Corinthians 12:12, KJV).

The Lord gave man these gifts to perform on the earth, but in order for us to do the work of God, it will take time to display it in our Christian life. When Jesus was on the earth, He performed so many miracles. Christians know that He performed miracles, but many will be surprised to learn of the amount. He also did many other things as well. If all the things that Jesus did on the earth were to be recorded, the whole world would not have room for the book that would be written.

DEALING WITH EVIL PEOPLE

When Jesus was on the earth, He performed many miracles, helped people, but at the same time, people had negative things to say about Him. He was stoned; they did all kinds of things to Him, but He kept on helping them. They will do the same thing to you and me, so we must stay in prayer. The Bible often warns us to avoid evil people or at least their bad behavior. God tells us to stay away and be very careful with those people who can destroy the life that He desires to create for us. Psalm 34:21 (KJV) says, "Evil shall slay the wicked: and they that hate the righteous shall be desolate."

First Peter 3:8-18 (ESV) tells us about evil people. He says,

> Finally, all of you, have unity of mind, sympathy, brotherly love, a tender heart, and a humble mind. Do not repay evil for evil or reviling for reviling, but on the contrary, bless, for to this you were called, that you may obtain a blessing. For whoever desires to love life and see good days, let him keep his tongue from evil and his lips from speaking deceit; let him turn away from evil and do good; let him seek peace and pursue it. For the eyes of the Lord are on the righteous, and his ears are open to their prayer. But the face of the Lord is against those who do evil.

Evil people always think that they are doing the right thing. They believe that their way is always right. We all know the first evil one, the devil, sinned from the beginning. So 1 John 3:8 told us that if it was not for the Bible, the origin of evil would remain unexplained. God is so good to us that He sent help, His Son Jesus. Today, I can say I am free with the blood of Jesus Christ. John 3:16 (KJV) told us, "For God so loved the world, that He gave his only begotten Son, that whosoever believeth in him should not perish, but have everlasting life."

God has spent a few thousand years doing this very thing! The story of Scripture is the story of God dealing with sinful people who hurt Him and others. He confronts sinful people and works with them, but ultimately, He draws the boundary and puts an end to it. He also separates Himself from sinful people and allows them to go their own way. He does not control them or force them to change. But He just refuses to engage in their sinful lifestyle. This is what I tell people every day when they come to me with trouble in their jobs or families. I do not tell them to try to win them over or change them in some way. I just tell them to do what God does, and what Jesus did, and what we are to do on the earth to help people around us.

I always encourage people in the church to love, be honest, and be kind to sinful people. Sometimes, you might never see them again. I was just describing the process of living in a world with sinful people. Some people do not want to hear about God, but at the same time, you are so kind to them and loving. It gets in their heart, and they cannot sleep at night. Your best defense against sinful people is to be like Apostle Paul and have a clear set time in your life, a time that no one can change. Paul talked to good people, the ones that gave him respect, and he enjoyed a good relationship with them. He also took a loving stand against sinful people. John 14:15 (ESV) says, "If you love me, you will keep my commandments." You can influence some sinful people to change their behavior, and they can enjoy a better life. Some sinful people will never move forward toward the life that God wants them to live. Some of those people never take the time to look into themselves. Psalm 37:2 (ESV) says, "For they will soon fade like the grass and wither like the green herb." Some people wake in the morning, start the day with a cup of coffee, never take the time to look back. I do not wake myself; it must be God.

God tells us about sinful people; He also makes a way for us to follow when we encounter sinful people. He tells us that if we follow His path, we will not only enjoy many good times, but some bad times will come, but God will be there to help us. It doesn't mean that we will walk away from those who are difficult or harmful. It means that in order for a transformation to take place, Christians have to work harder for a sinner to change. We must not nag them or ignore them or attempt to control their sinful nature; take a stand and refuse to participate in their sinful life. Be an honest and loving person of God, stay in the light by living out good values and kindly taking a stand against sinful people. Sometimes, you will face problems, but let the sinful person know that this is how the world wakes up. If that person knows something about the world, he or she will be wise and change from a sinful lifestyle, give their heart to God, and both of you will have a good relationship.

The Bible informs us and also gives us some instructions on how to deal with sinful people and their problems, and He also gave us the information to determine what kind of sinful person we are dealing with when we face this sinful world. Luke 17:3-4 (KJV) says,

> Take heed to yourselves: If thy brother trespass against thee, rebuke him; and if he repent, forgive him. And if he trespass against thee seven times in a day, and seven times in a day turn again to thee, saying, I repent; thou shalt forgive him.

We will encounter sinful people, but we have to forgive them. Remember, we are children of the Most High God. There is a very important message in this verse. We can help someone to change their sinful ways and forgive their enemy.

When you have a relationship with God, He will let you know that you are wrong with that person. If you apologize to that person and he repents and changes his or her mind, forgive them. If that person is willing to go forward, pray and make a visible effort to change whatever they have done to you; forgive them because the Bible says so. A sinful person can change if he wants. "Thou wast perfect in thy ways from the day that thou wast created, till iniquity found in thee" (Ezekiel 28:15, KJV).

At times, people will think of the other as a sinner, but if that person prays to God for forgiveness and repents, God can use him in a mighty way. Everyone on this earth needs to forgive and be forgiven in order to have a relationship with God. The Bible tells us about reconciliation, but in order for us to engage in the restoration of friendly relations, we have to forgive the other. And when we forgive that person, I hope that person admits that he or she was wrong and makes a positive change in life. It is good to forgive someone, but there are some people out there who, when forgiven, refuse to change their bad behavior. "I acknowledged my sin unto thee, and mine iniquity have I not hid. I said, I will confess my transgressions unto the LORD: and thou forgavest the iniquity of my sin" (Psalm 32:5, KJV).

My pastor told us dealing with sinful people can be a problem. Be prepared to encounter a lot of resistance, arguments, justifications, excuses, and attacks. Brace yourself, learn how to accept the problem and the territory that come with Christianity. Pray and ask God to help you because it is not your job to fix it. Sometimes, it can cause a confrontation between you and someone who is not a Christian.

DUE HONOR TO PARENTS

Parenting can let you know who God is because when having a problem with kids, God is the One who steps in to help you. If you want to be a good parent, you have to give a great part of yourself in order to raise your children to become loving, responsible adults. Parents give their heart, soul, mind, and strength just to see their children reach their gold in life. At the same time, parenting can constantly bring us down to let us face our own inadequacies and make us aware of our humanity.

I can remember the night when my daughter had an ear infection. She was crying so badly; I can only imagine the excruciating pain she was going through. Her mother and I knew we had to get her to the emergency room immediately. Shevonnia was five years old; she was also diagnosed with autism. Her mother said, "Let's hurry," and secured her in the back seat of the car. The hospital was about twenty-five miles away, the weather was bad.

Driving that night was so hard because slush was on the ground, and my mind was running all over the place. That night was a nightmare; I tried to look through the rearview mirror to see if she was okay. I tried to talk to her, but she did not respond to me. Some doctors say that untreated ear infections can lead to more serious complications, including mastoiditis (a rare inflammation of a bone adjacent to the ear). It seemed like it was just yesterday. A long drive still brings this memory to my mind. The sickness of my daughter made me realize how God is good to us. As we go through the hard times in life, God always sets a time for us because there is nothing on this earth that can happen to us before the time. I am here to let you know that there is a set time in your life, a time that no one can change.

BEING A GOOD PARENT

The Bible tells us that being a good parent can be a difficult and challenging venture, but at the same time, it can be the most rewarding and fulfilling thing we will ever do. The Bible has a great deal to say about the way we can successfully raise our children to be men and women of God. As good parents, the first thing we must do is teach them the truth about God's Word.

Along with loving God and being a godly example by committing ourselves to His commands, we need to heed the command of Deuteronomy 6:7 (KJV): "And thou shalt teach them diligently unto thy children, and shalt take of them when thou sittest in thine home, and when thou walkest by the way, and when thou liest dawn, and when thou risest up," regarding teaching our children to do the same. This passage emphasizes the ongoing nature of such instruction. It should be done at all times—at home, on the road, at night, and in the morning. Biblical truth should be the foundation of our homes. By following the principles of these commands, we teach our children that worshiping God should be constant, not reserved for Sunday mornings or Saturday nightly prayers.

Although our children learn a great deal through direct teaching, they learn much more by watching us. This is why we must be careful in everything we do. We must first acknowledge our God-given roles. Husbands and wives are to be mutually respectful and submissive to each other. Ephesians 5:21 (KJV) says, "Submitting yourselves one to another in the fear of God." At the same time, God has established a line of authority to keep order. "I want you to realize that the head of every man is Christ, and the head of the woman is man, and the head of Christ is God" (1 Corinthians 11:3, NIV). We know that Christ is not inferior to God, just as a wife is not inferior to her husband. God recognizes, however, that without submission to authority, there is no order. The husband's responsibility as the head of the household is to love his wife as he loves his own body in the same sacrificial way that Christ loved the church (Ephesians 5:25). In response to this loving leadership, it is not difficult for the wife to submit to her husband's authority. Ephesians 5:24 (KJV) says, "Therefore as the church is subject unto Christ, so let the wives be to their own husbands in everything." Colossians 3:18 (KJV) says, "Wives, submit yourselves unto your own husbands, as unto the Lord." Her primary responsibility is to love and respect her husband, live in wisdom and purity, and take care of the home. "That they may teach the young women to be sober, to love their husbands, to love their children (Titus 2:4, KJV). Women are naturally more nurturing than men because they were designed to be the primary caretakers of their children.

Discipline and instruction are integral parts of being a good parent. Proverbs 13:24 (BSB) says, "He who spares the rod hates his son, but he who loves him disciplines him diligently." Children who grow up in undisciplined households feel unwanted and unworthy. They lack direction and self-control, and as they get older, they rebel and have little or no respect for any kind of authority, including God's. "Chasten thy son while there is hope, and let not thy soul spare for his crying" (Proverbs 19:18, KJV). At the same time, discipline must be balanced with love, or children may grow up resentful, discouraged, and rebellious. Colossians 3:21 (KJV) says, "Fathers, provoke not your children to anger, lest they be discouraged." God recognizes that discipline is painful when it is happening (Hebrews 12:11), but if followed by loving instruction, it is remarkably beneficial to the child. "Fathers, do not exasperate your children; instead, bring them up in the training and instruction of the Lord" (Ephesians 6:4, NIV).

Parent of All Parents

When God created us, He has a responsibility to take care of us. He is the parent of all parents, but being a parent is not an easy job. Sometimes, the kids get out of hand. And as a parent, He has to help us and show us the right way to go. He parents us so that we will help other kids and adults. He helps us grow up in the spiritual so that the reason He says, "Train up your child in the way he should go: and when he is old, he will not depart from it" (Proverbs 22:6, KJV). He also tells us how to act like a kid because when you are an adult, you cannot act like a kid. He raises us in a way for us to accomplish His purposes. As parents, we take on the burden of representing God and His ways to our children. God knows that we cannot do it ourselves, so He put His Holy Spirit into us to direct us. We know that He has the resources to help us, so we humble ourselves in Him. I think that every parent should have a relationship with God because being a parent does not come with a handbook. You have to depend on God to give you the guidance to do the job.

Parenting in the spiritual should be the same in the natural. We should have a heart like God to raise kids. Deuteronomy 6:6, 11:19 (KJV) says,

> These words, which I command thee this day, shall be in thine heart: And thou shalt teach them diligently unto thy children. Ye shall teach them to your children, speaking of them when thou sittest in thine house, and when thou walkest by the way, when thou liest down, and when thou risest up.

These are some good words to encourage your kids in God; when newborn babies come into this world, they learn to trust their parents. As they grow, you have to let them learn to trust God. Your earthly parents will give you clothes, a roof over your head, and also food on your table, but your heavenly Parent will give you enteral life. Hebrews 12:6 (KJV) says, "For whom the Lord loveth He chasteneth, and scourgeth every son whom he receiveth." As a parent, you have to help your child grow in Christ; you have to give them the necessary things to go forward in life because there is a time coming that no one can stop you, a time that God ordained, and that is a set time.

PACK THEM AND STACK THEM

Every parent would like to see their children come out good in life. Some parents go to the extremes to provide an environment that will help their children enter this world and achieve their goals. Every parent must create an independent, strong foundation for their children in order for them to grow into adults. It will take a lot of work, but the goal is to pack them and stack them so that they can accomplish the tasks, duties, and responsibilities of life on their own without being dependent on the resources of their parent. Luke 2:40 (KJV) says, "And the child grew, and waxed strong in spirit, filled with wisdom: and the grace of God was upon him."

Every child that God put on this earth needs guidance. They cannot function on their own. Some of them think that they can function on their own, but when it comes to the end of the rope, they cry to their parents for help. Some kids do not possess the ability to manage life and the problems that come with it. A good parent takes the time to teach his or her child the right way to go because that child has not experienced the fact of life. That parent must provide love, kindness and tell the child the truth and all the other things that will help this child develop the ability to face life. The Bible tells us that we should pray for parents, "O my lord, […] teach us what we shall do unto the child that shall be born" (Judges 13:8, KJV). I think that when a child is born, the parent should look to the Lord for help because that child did not come with a guideline.

Isaiah 54:13 (KJV) tells us, "All thy children shall be taught of the LORD: and great shall be the peace of thy children."

When a child is getting ready to get married and leave their mother and father, give them your blessing. The Bible tells us that in Matthew 19:5 (NIV), "For this reason a man will leave his father and mother and be united to his wife, and the two will become one flesh."

The role of a parent is not easy; this role has a lot of different personality traits, the combination of different characteristics that a parent demonstrates. The sleepless nights, crying, and sometimes laughing, but the most difficult aspect of all is the ending of the job. Some parents cannot wait for their child to grow up, but when they do, the parent's mind is all over the place, thinking about them. When being asked about raising children, some parents think for a moment and say it is God. When the kid is no longer living with you, and they can function on their own, you feel successful and say your job is well done.

When a child enters this world, it will take a lot of help for them to survive, so God put people in different places to help them. God said, "Suffer little children [...] come onto me" (Matthew 19:14, KJV) just to show the world that God cares for children. The plan that God has for parents is for them to constantly work hard in order for their child to survive. What I am trying to say: when a kid leaves home, you pack them and stack them, and he or she should be no longer dependent on you emotionally or financially. That kid has reached the age to know that God can help him anywhere that he chooses to go in life. The Bible describes it this way, "The fear of the LORD is the beginning of wisdom: a good understanding have all they that do his commandments" (Psalm 111:10, KJV).

Years ago, I was invited to a wedding. Everyone was having a good time, so a good friend of mine came to me and said the groom's mother was crying. My wife went over to her just to comfort her. She told my wife, "It is not easy to see your kid go." In my mind, I was saying, "You need to let go of your kids and let them get the experiences of life." It is a challenge for some parents. Their whole heart was in their kids and the relationship that they shared. One lady turned to my wife and said, "I have a deep and loving feeling toward all my children. It is hard to let go." The relationship between parents and children is very important because some parents invest a lot in their kids, and some feel like the kids are supposed to stay with them all their lives. Some parents raise their kids to take care of them when they get old, and when life does not go the way it was planned, parents have a problem and disown their child.

Being a parent is not easy. You will face things out of the norm, and sometimes, you will say that the child is not yours. According to the wise man Solomon, "Even a child is known by his doings, whether his work be pure, and whether it be right" (Proverbs 20:11, KJV). Sometimes, when a father does not acknowledge his child, it will turn out that the same child will have to help the father in his old age. Most of the time, some kids love their mother more than their father; that is something I try to understand. The reason why I say that: on Father's Day, it is so calm, and the restaurants are empty. When it comes to Mother's Day, all the restaurants are full; there is no way to park; everyone is so busy.

There is something that caught my attention: some parents work hard and take care of their children. Some of those children grow up to be very successful, and the kids abandon their parents. A mother is like the ground of the earth: she produces everything for her child in order for the child to go forward in life. Those characteristics of parents, and my parents demonstrated these characteristics. They worked very hard for us, and today I am proud of them. The Bible says the hand that rocks the cradle is the hand that rules the world.

This agrees with the saying of the wise man, "Train up a child in the way he should go: and when he is old, he will not depart from it" (Proverbs 22:6, KJV). The fact is parents are so strong. They carry the weight of the world on their shoulders and burdens of pain in their hearts. Some parents said, "I cannot wait until my kids leave the house," but I would like to share this with you: the job of a parent never ends. My mother was always telling me, "When they are small, they tangle your foot, and when they are adults, they tangle your heart."

Teaching Your Child

It was not easy to understand the big picture of parenting, but let us take your attention to some lessons to learn in order for them to go through life. These lessons are not hard, but your child needs to learn them. These lessons will take them throughout childhood, from infancy to the teen years. The beauty of parenting is there are some areas that you have the ability to be dealing with all the time. In order for you to knowledge all these areas, you will need wisdom, observation, prayer, and the support of others who are willing to help and share. It is very important to let your child know that sharing is a part of growing up in the Lord. God teaches us to share with others, just like He did with people on the earth. He set the example for you and me to follow. John 3:16 (KJV) says, "For God so loved the world, that he gave his only begotten Son, that whosoever believeth in him should not perish, but have everlasting life." Sharing can be described in many different ways. The first way is reaching outside of ourselves to help someone.

Take the initiative to respond to someone who is having a bad day or has no food on the table.

Parents must take the time out to teach their children the ways of life so that nothing takes them by surprise. Start to teach your child from the womb, and he or she will become a happy child from birth and as he or she matures and becomes a teen. Solomon shared what his father did for him as a child. "He taught me also, and said unto me, Let thine heart retain my words: keep my commandments, and live" (Proverbs 4:4, KJV). We must teach our children how to detect things emotionally by teaching them what to expect when they reach out for love and the wrong thing happens. Children need to know that things won't always work in their favor. The things they want someone else wants too. It is good to let our kids know all of this. It is simple to us, but it is not simple to them. God designed your kids to know all of this. It is good to provide them with food, clothing, housing, and protection, but what happens when their hearts get broken. You think your presence will help take care of their emotional problem; they have to be taught how to deal with relationships. Every time your baby boy or girl reaches out his or her arms, you are there. If your little girl cries in school all day, you should listen to her and give her an answer. When your teenage son is having problems with another student, you are there to guide him in coming up with a solution to the problem.

When your child learns how to reach out to others for the rest of their life, they will need many experiences in order for them to go forward in life. Love and support are very important for children's growth. Now, your growing kids can go out there and make friends with anyone and everyone, with love. Some parents take their kids around the world and let them meet different people of different nationalities. The reason children would be able to interact with a variety of people is because they have been exposed and have seen that there are people out there that love them just like their parents. Finally, all parents should teach their children the things of God. Deuteronomy 6:7, 11:19 says,

> Thou shalt teach them diligently unto thy children. Ye shall teach them your children, speaking of them when thou sittest in thine house, and when thou walkest by the way when thou liest down, and when thou risest up.

Your Personal Attitude toward Truth

What does the word "truth" mean to you? I believe that there are almost as many answers to that question as there are people who answer it. People have said there is no such thing as a half-truth. Some people refuse to talk the truth because they do not get the recognition they want, so they tell lies to look good all the time. Second Thessalonians 2:10-12 (KJV) says,

> Because they received not the love of the truth, that they might be saved. And for this cause God shall send them strong delusion, that they should believe a lie: That they all might be damned who believed not the truth, but has pleasure in unrighteousness.

Only the truth shall set you free. Only when you follow God's commandments will He help you to go forward in life. The more we talk about truth, the more a lie seems to lose its meaning. Sometimes, when we talk, we cannot draw a contrast because it is difficult to know if we are talking about the same thing since the truth is good and the lie is bad. From the beginning, we experience the growth of grace and the attitude of love. Second Thessalonians 2:13 (KJV) tells us that "God hath from the beginning chosen you for salvation through sanctification of the Spirit and belief of the truth."

The Bible tells us about the truth. How many of us practice it and live a life according to the truth? Second Timothy 4:3-4 (KJV) says,

For the time will come when they will not endure sound doctrine; but after their own lusts shall they heap to themselves teachers, having itching ears; and they shall turn away their ears from the truth, and shall be turned unto fables.

Some people have problems with the truth. The fact still remains; the truth will never change. You may lie more than one time, but the truth is still the same. If I could sum up the truth in one statement, I would start like this: God loves you just the way you are, but He refuses to leave you that way. He wants you to be just like Jesus.

Psalm 89:14 (NCV) says, "Your kingdom is built on what is right and fair. Love and truth are in all you do." To tell the truth is always good. Some people think that because they are in a bad situation, they should tell a lie. The truth should always be told because God honors the truth. The Bible recognizes the truth, and the truth will be for all ages and will be for every generation. Second Peter 1:12 (KJV) says, "Wherefore I will not be negligent to put you always in remembrance of these things, though ye know them, and be established in the present truth." When you live your life in a mature way, the lie is no longer a part of you; the truth takes over your body and gets you ready for the kingdom of heaven. When you reach the age of maturity, you think differently. You also study the Word of God in a different way. There is something about maturity. It causes you to approach life differently. If some part of your life is out of control and results in negative consequences, you may be struggling with the truth. If so, you are a pathological liar. Here are some steps that you can take to grow up. Remember where God brought you from. Be more mature in your spirit. You will see God start to make a change in your life. First, you have to admit to yourself, to God, and to another person that you are a liar and that it is getting the best of you. In admitting that you are powerless on your own to fix it, ask God for forgiveness for the things that you have said and claim it. Receive it and start to tell the truth.

Believe that God can help you. Reach out to Him and totally submit yourself to His care. Let Him know the person you are: a man with clean lips and hands. Remember to submit to Him in obedience and ask Him to show you how to stay in maturity. Sometimes, people say things that are not true. I wish that if they could take an ongoing inventory of themselves and apologize to the people that they lied to. I pray that some people stay in prayer continually and ask God to show them the way to stop lying. Go and ask for forgiveness; go to the people you lied to and who you hurt and tell them that you have harmed them. At the same time, seek God deeply, ask Him what He wants you to do, let Him know that you want to stop doing the things you are doing. Stay in prayer and reach out to others because of the things you have said.

This kind of behavior is in the world today. People use lies as a business. It does not matter how much the job is paying you to lie. Remember that God does not like liars.

> Why is my language not clear to you? Because you are unable to hear what I say. You belong to your father, the devil, and you want to carry out your father's desires. He was a murderer from the beginning, not holding to the truth, for there is no truth in him. When he lies, he speaks his native language, for he is a liar and the father of lies. Yet because I tell the truth, you do not believe me! Can any of you prove me guilty of sin? If I am telling the truth, why don't you believe me? Whoever belongs to God hears what God says. The reason you do not hear is that you do not belong to God.

> John 8:43-47 (NIV)

When you are a liar, you are working for the devil, but one day, you will get your payday.

Fulfill Your Dreams

"For God so loved the world, that he gave his only begotten Son, that whosoever believeth in him should not perish, but have everlasting life" (John 3:16, KJV). Thank God for His Son. We cannot make it on our own. His love, His tender mercy, and His progressive sanctification are with us as long as we live. Keep the faith strong because God is with you, and all your dreams will be fulfilled. God will set a time in your life that no human being can change, and that is a set time. You may go through some things in your life, but when God says it is finished, it is all over, "Power belongs to Me." In the book of Job, he went through some mush, but when God says your time has come, it is finished. God gave Job more than what he lost. Christians should be aware that bad times will come, but when God says it is finished, God will take over from there.

One man inspires me so much. His name is Tyler Perry. One day, as I went inside the house, the TV was on. Someone was interviewing him. He talked about his life as a child. Tyler Perry told many things about his family lifestyle, and today, he has a great success in life to show the world. When God says it is finished, no man on earth can stop you from going forward in life. Today I am here to encourage all people never to give up. You may go through bad times in your life, but there is a time coming, and that is a set time. The reason why Tyler Perry is successful is because God set a time in his life that no man can change. He is always helping someone keep up the good work; Tyler Perry, God bless you. The book of Job tells us that we will engage in problems, but God will always be there for us:

Behold, happy is the man whom God correcteth: therefore, despise not thou the chastening of the Almighty: for he maketh sore, and bindeth up: he woundeth, and his hands make whole. He shall deliver thee in six troubles: yea, in seven there shall no evil touch thee.

Job 5:17-19 (KJV)

God is so good to us; we must remember where He took us from and keep us in the land of the living.

Truth and Maturity

Throughout the ages, God has put people in our life to encourage us. He is telling us that He is with us. His Word never changes. His words are eternal. Look back at the history of God, the full story of His people, and how they followed His path, and in doing so, have hope, blessing, transformation, and much more. There will come a time when you stay in the presence of God. His manifestation will start to embody you and take you to the next level. God shows us many ways He engages in our lives and moves among us as we continue to lift up His name in prayer. When we pray, He hears our prayer, and He transforms us, the ones that earnestly seek His face. The Bible tells us about Daniel. He prayed many times a day. Daniel also had dreams and visions. Daniel 7:1 tells us that "Daniel had a dream and visions of his head upon his bed: then he wrote the dream, and told the sum of the matters."

> And we know that all things work together for good to those who love God, to those who are the called according to His purpose. For whom He foreknew, He also predestined to be conformed to the image of His Son [...] If God be for us, who can be against us?

> Romans 8:28-29 (KJV)

God calls us His children, and He will do everything to win us back to Him.

First Corinthians 6:20 (KJV) says, "For ye are bought with a price: therefore glorify God in your body, and in your spirit, which are God's." So, as children of God, we must wake up and give the devil a fight. We must stand up proud and take back what the evil one has stolen away from us. We must pray so God can put Himself on exhibition in our life. Because Christ is the sum of all spiritual things, if we ask for anything in His name, He will give it to us.

Stay Strong in the Lord

The Lord told us that He will never leave us or forsake us. A good friend of mine, whose name I will not mention, told me a story that made my relationship with the Lord stronger. He told the story in the church of when he came to the USA. It was so hard for him, but he put Christ first in his life. He became a Christian, engaged in the Word of God, and attended church very regularly, but everything was going bad for him. However, he remembered that God said He will never leave us. He told us that he worked for a company. The company hired him before checking his papers. On the weekend, the boss came up to him and said, "I am not paying you because your papers are not good." He cried and left. He could not pay his rent or buy food. The landlord put him out. He was living on the street. One of his church brothers helped him get a driving job. God was so good to him. Psalm 116:12 (KJV) says, "What shall I render unto the Lord for all his benefits toward me?" From there, God kept on blessing him. He went to college to get his master's degree and started to preach the gospel.

When I look back at his story, I remember the story of Joseph. Joseph went through hard times in his life, but God was with him. We all know the story of Joseph, the part that caught my attention is when he said, "You intended to harm me, but God intended it for good, [...] the saving of many lives" (Genesis 50:20, NIV). There was a time in Joseph's life when everything was going wrong, and at the same time, he was faithful as an employee. As a capable administrator, he always believed that one day, God would change things around. He was waiting on his time to come. Isaiah 40:31

(KJV) says, "But they that wait upon the LORD shall renew their strength; they shall mount up with wings as eagles; they shall run, and not be weary; and they shall walk, and not faint." He looked at it as a training program in the pits and the prisons. He never gave up. He believed in a set time, a time when no one can stop you. He knew that God is in control of the circumstances. Your time is not God's time. A songwriter said, "I am next in line for my blessing."

Joseph looked back at where God took him from and realized that he had no control over his life. All he knew was that God had a special plan for his life, and when his time came, he finally accessed the opportunity and moved forward in life. When God's hands are on you, He has a special job for you. Joseph went through a lot, and he accomplished a lot. He moved from being a shepherd to being the primary administrator for the pharaoh. He is also the king's right-hand man. God can take you places you cannot imagine. You are just as special in God's eyes as Joseph was. God predestined Joseph for that time. That time was a set time when no one could stop him. No one could kill him because that time was a set time in his life. If God could keep Joseph for a time like that, He can do the same thing for you, so stay in Christ and give Him all the glory. Do you think God has predestined you for a special time in your life? If so, tell yourself you are not going to the grave with this talent.

Biblical history is filled with the stories of people who have sought to follow the Lord, and in the end, they triumphed over their enemies. Some of them went through many problems, lost their family, and got sick along the way, but at the same time, God gave them the blessing of hope and healing. It is not different in today's life. Stay with God, and He will take care of you. The spirit of the Lord lives and moves among His children. He transforms those who stay at the foot of the cross. As you started to read this book, you might have said to yourself, "When is my time?" Everyone has a set time. You may be going through some struggles, but your time is coming.

The Bible tells us about Esther, the little Jew girl, who was carried away from Jerusalem. She had no mother and no father. Just imagine how she felt. It might have been hard for her, but her time was coming. Mordecai was the only family she had. When the king was choosing a wife, Esther was among the girls. We all know the story, but to show you that it does not matter where you are or what circumstances you are in: when God says this is your time, no one can stop you. Esther received high favor over all the girls. Esther served the Jewish family, the same lineage Jesus Christ came from. As we follow the life of Esther, we will see how God can use people to change things around in some people's life. When you read, you will see how they appear. Some of the principles stay in the chronological order in which they happened; some appeared much later in her growth process. We can understand that God's time is different from our time, and we will see the miraculous work of God's principles unfold. When these miraculous transformations take place, you will see the power of God at work. Each one happened to show us that God can use anyone. When all of these principles happen, you will see how God can transform a little Jewish girl to become queen.

When Esther became queen, all of hell's doors opened. She had work to do. The Bible tells us that when Mordecai was in trouble, Esther prayed to God for help. Today, you and I can follow that same principle to reach out to God for help. She also took the initiative to see the king in a time of trouble. When God places us in a family, it is for us to help the family go forward in life. Sometimes, we curse our families because of the way they act, but Esther did not do that. She was placed in that position to help the Jewish people. When Haman was trying to kill Mordecai, God turned it around. What a mighty God we serve. He promised to never leave us or forsake us. All these things happened through one little Jewish girl who was taken from Jerusalem. Today, I would like to encourage you: when the Lord put you somewhere, take it as an honor because He wants to do work through you. Remember your families. It does not matter how they look or how they behave. Pray for them because God will allow you to be the cornerstone in that family. In the book of Esther, she did not know all the Jewish people that came from Jerusalem, but she prayed for all of them. It did not take long for me to understand why Esther was put out so much. She knew that a day would come when they would kill her because of her Jewish culture.

BIBLIOGRAPHY

Akoa-Mongo, François Kara. *Sermons (125) Preached from the Pulpit of Machiasport, Maine: 1991-2010*. Bloomington: Trafford Publishing, 2011.

Alves, Elizabeth. *Becoming a Prayer Warrior*. Ada: Baker Books, 2003.

Brown, William D. "One & Two." SermonCentral. October 11, 2011. https://www.sermoncentral.com/sermons/2-one-two-william-d-brown-sermon-on-greatness-161325.

Cloud, Henry. *God Will Make a Way: What to Do When You Don't Know What to Do*. Nashville: Thomas Nelson Inc., 2006.

Cloud, Henry, and John Townsend. *God Will Make a Way: What to Do When You Don't Know What to Do*. Nashville: Thomas Nelson, 2006.

Cloud, Henry, and John Townsend. *What to Do When You Don't Know What to Do: Sex and Intimacy*. Nashville: Thomas Nelson, 2005.

Houdmann, S. Michael. *Got Questions? Bible Questions Answered—Answers to the Questions People Are Really Asking*. Bloomington: WestBow Press, 2014.

Lucado, Max. *Traveling Light Journal*. Nashville: Thomas Nelson, 2001.

Meyer, Joyce. *Let God Fight Your Battles: Being Peaceful in the Storm*. London: Hachette UK, 2015.

Meyer, Joyce. *The Battle Belongs to the Lord: Overcoming Life's Struggles through Worship*. London: Hachette UK, 2008.

RailHopeSA Committee. "About Us: RailHope South Africa." Rail-Hope South Africa. http://railhopesouthafrica.co.za/About-Us.

Religiousbeliefs, "The 9 Gifts of the Holy Spirit." Opera News. https://ng.opera.news/ng/en/religion/71711695a099d-89d1e3b14dbf60445ff.

Shipe, Christy. "What Does the Bible Say about Drinking Alcohol?" Crosswalk. March 2, 2021. https://www.crosswalk.com/faith/spiritual-life/what-does-the-bible-say-about-alcohol-1120038.html.

Summers, Ray. *Worthy Is the Lamb*. Nashville: B&H Publishing Group, 1999.

Tyme, "Prayer is our only means of communicating with God. when you pray, pray like this." Opera News. https://ng.opera.news/ng/en/religion/6a74f8a1e56545ee34e2b90baf1a5954.

Watch Tower Bible. "What Is Forgiveness? The Bible's answer." https://wol.jw.org/en/wol/d/r1/lp-e/502015232.

Words of Life Ministries. "Study 5: What to Do with Life's Burdens." https://www.wordsoflife.co.uk/bible-studies/study-5-what-to-do-with-lifes-burdens.

About the Author

John Henry was born in Jamaica, West Indies. He migrated to the United States of America. He came to realize life is nothing unless God is in it. He believes in going out to preach to a dying world. This is Mr. Henry's first book. He feels that God instilled something in him to write many more books. *A Set Time in Your Life* will help you be patient and wait on the Lord.